Advance Praise for *Your Best Digital Life*

"The best way to get more value from the digital age is not by upgrading our technology. Instead, we need to upgrade our psychology to make better use of the technology we already have. It has taken me decades to learn the eye-opening lessons you will find in this book."

—RORY SUTHERLAND, author of *Alchemy* and vice chairman at Ogilvy

"A timely guide to reclaiming inner freedom by guiding our digital habits with intention. Essential for anyone seeking to inhabit their Being, rather than letting technology dictate unconscious habit patterns."

—Nipun Mehta, founder, ServiceSpace

"We all know that our smartphones and social media are eating our brains, but fighting back often feels impossible (and besides, FOMO). In this hopeful and practical book, Jonathan Garner and Menka Sanghvi show how you can rethink and redesign your digital life and offer step-by-step guidance to mobilize your attention, observe your behavior, reflect on your action and experiment with new tools and habits to build your best digital life."

—Alex Soojung-Kim Pang, author of *The Distraction Addiction*, *Rest* and *Work Less, Do More*

"Entrepreneurs often face tech overload. Garner and Sanghvi provide a masterclass in using digital tools without letting them take over your life."

—Andy Budd, author of *The Growth Equation*

"The list of challenges related to our digital devices goes on and on—as do all the manuals and blogs devoted to 'fixing' these problems. But Garner and Sanghvi's book really cuts through, not just because their 'M.O.R.E.' method is highly memorable and effective in shifting our digital habits, but because it's grounded in principles of growth and exploration that apply equally to so many other aspects of our daily lives."

—Dan Nixon, author of *The Perpetual Beginner* on Substack

"Imagine leaving your phone at home next time you go for a walk, to work or to meet a friend for a coffee. What you are feeling now is why everyone needs this book."

—Ryan Hopkins, author of *52 Weeks of Wellbeing*

YOUR BEST DIGITAL LIFE

Use your mind to tame your tech

JONATHAN GARNER
MENKA SANGHVI

ILLUSTRATIONS BY GREG CLARKE

For the benefit of all minds living in this digital age.

Contents

Part 1: Principles
Guiding Principles to Live a Better Digital Life

Part 2: Method
A Simple Way to Apply the Principles

Part 3: Practice
Using the M.O.R.E. Method in Your Best Digital Life

Foreword

I first met Jonathan back in March of 2022 at the Sync Digital Wellbeing Summit, one of the world's biggest conferences on the topic. We were both invited to join an eclectic roster of speakers that included prominent psychologists, neuroscientists, policymakers and thought leaders—including authors such as James Clear (*Atomic Habits*) and Simon Sinek (*Start with Why*). Over two thrilling days, we were immersed in scientific insights and theories about how technology shapes our lives—for better or worse.

During one of the breaks, I was queuing up for a coffee in the speakers' area, where I struck up a conversation with Jonathan. Before long, he handed me a small box with just three words printed on the front: Digital Habit Lab. Opening it up, I found a deck of beautifully illustrated cards, each describing a practical experiment designed to help people become more intentional with their tech use. I started to read one of these cards and intuitively began to think about how I could implement it.

At that moment, a light bulb went off in my head—while there was lots of great theory being discussed on the stage, it often felt overwhelming and difficult to know what to do with it. Yet here in my hand was a simple tool that anyone could use to immediately begin reshaping their relationship with technology.

As I fanned out the cards and slowly looked through them, Jonathan explained that he had developed them through his company, Mind over Tech, with the help of talented collaborators, including the mindfulness expert Menka Sanghvi. As we continued to speak, it became clear to me that they had dedicated an enormous amount of time to figuring out not only how we can reduce our unhealthy reliance on technology but also, crucially, how we can transform the time we spend with our devices into an opportunity for serious personal growth. I was blown away by the potential in what I saw and invited Jonathan to join me on my podcast to dig in deeper.

Clearly, I wasn't the only one impressed by their unique approach. Six months later—following a successful Kickstarter launch of the card deck—I was in touch with Jonathan again. He told me he'd been approached by a publisher that was interested in him writing a book about digital well-being but that he wasn't sure whether a long-form book would be the right format for making an impact. From our conversation on the podcast, however, I knew there was so much more nuance to explore, particularly when it came to the messy reality of applying these experiments in everyday life. A book would be a chance to present not just the experiments but the "why" behind them all. So I encouraged Jonathan to join forces with Menka and get their ideas into a book. To be honest, I wasn't sure if they would do it, but I really hoped they would.

To my delight, they embraced the challenge! And now, I have the privilege of writing this foreword for what has turned out to be an important book for our times. Jonathan and Menka have crafted an inspiring call to action by taking leading scientific research and insights and translating them into a practical four-step methodology. And just to make sure you're not left wondering where to start, they show you exactly how to apply this methodology in six key practices in your digital life. This book has made a genuinely positive shift in my own digital habits, and I am confident that you, too, will find it of immense value.

—Mo Gawdat
ex-chief business officer for Google X and author of *Solve for Happy*
Dubai, September 2024

Introduction
Or, What This Book Is and Why It'll Help You

The average person spends roughly 30 percent of their waking life using their smartphone. Add in the time spent with all our other digital tech, and that's the significant "digital life" this book is about. And yet, so much of our digital behavior happens by accident, either not being aware of our actions or not feeling in control of them.

Most advice on this subject is based on reducing and restricting the time spent on digital devices, but this doesn't get to the root of the problem. Living your best digital life is about making sure each moment spent with them contributes to the things that matter to you most.

This book proposes a radically different, mind-first approach to working with your digital habits, based on insights from neuroscience, psychology and contemplative practices. We will share a method that doesn't rely on willpower alone. When applied properly, it transforms your tech from a source of distraction into a tool that helps you accomplish more of the things you care about.

Who Is This Book For?

Digital well-being is a hot topic, and there is a lot of advice out there. But if you've ever tried implementing the proposed strategies, you know exactly what the challenge is: long-term sustainability once the initial enthusiasm has worn off. We all know reducing notifications, charging your phone outside your bedroom and deleting unhelpful apps can make a difference— yet few of us do all these things consistently. A major focus of this book is not to list more and more life hacks but rather to teach you how to work differently with your mind to start actually putting the ones you've already heard about into practice.

You should read this book if:

- You feel your relationship with technology is limiting your productivity, well-being and connection to yourself and others—and you want that to change.
- You have already tried any number of tips, tricks, hacks, secret methods and too-good-to-be-true solutions that lived up to their name, and you're unhappy with the results.
- You are invested in long-term behavior change and (this is key) are ready to do the work of looking inward, acknowledging the role you play in your relationship with your tech.

What You'll Learn From This Book

This book is divided into three parts:

Part 1: Principles

We share three core principles that challenge the way you think about your relationship with technology. These insights will create a foundational way to think about what your best digital life could look like.

Part 2: Method

We then teach you our tried-and-tested M.O.R.E. Method, a practical way to keep your digital habits working for you over time. These four simple steps boil the big ideas of Part 1 into a simple practice that you can begin immediately and continue perfecting over time.

Ultimately, it can be applied to your relationship with all tech—even future products that have not been invented yet. Whether that's a productivity app powered by AI, augmented reality glasses that record all your conversations or translation headphones that help you understand what your pets are saying, you can rely on the M.O.R.E. Method to help navigate the inevitable challenges they present and build a set of digital habits that best serve you.

Part 3: Practice
Finally, we delve into the possibilities for what a best digital life could look like. We explore six different areas that are widely considered the six pillars of well-being (PERMAH). What could your best digital life look like when it comes to your health, emotions or relationships? How can the M.O.R.E. Method be applied to these core areas of your life?

Each of these Practice chapters can stand alone, so you can read them sequentially or jump into whichever feels most relevant to you right now.

Why Should You Trust Us?

A fair question. We don't take your attention for granted. We know it's the most precious thing in the world (we've written a whole chapter about this: See Practice 2!), so we want this book to be as helpful as possible. Here are three reasons you should trust us to help you with your digital habits:

1. We Immensely Value Our Tech
We understand that flushing your phone down the toilet isn't a viable way to live in today's world. Not only is tech a necessary part of modern life, but we also believe it is desirable. Both of us have technology backgrounds. Before setting up Mind over Tech, a pioneering company that focuses on how to embrace technology with intention, Jonathan designed and delivered digital training workshops to leadership teams at some of the most successful companies in the world, many of them undergoing digital transformations. For over a decade, Menka worked on social innovation programs for global charities, looking for ways to leverage the latest tech (such as 3D printing and solar-powered water purification), often amazed at the profound role that tech can play in improving lives.

We deeply appreciate the power that technology gives us, individually and collectively. Whether it's the whole internet in your pocket or simply a killer app that can help you grocery shop while you're waiting in the school parking lot before pickup time, we love technology. We just want to ensure that it's working for us, in a way that works for us, rather than molding our lives in a way that changes who we are.

2. We Are Seasoned Meditators

Both of us take observing the workings of the mind very seriously. Steeped in contemplative traditions, we have both been meditating and working with (and on) our mental habits for decades. In fact, we first met in 2017 on a mindful photography walk that Menka had organized in London's South Bank. Once we got chatting, we realized both of us had recently been on meditation retreats where we spent a lot of our quiet time craving our smartphones (Jonathan confessed to hiding in a bathroom at one point to check his phone). How crazy is it, we thought, that even when we're in an environment that we've chosen to be in, perfectly designed to help us observe and still our minds, we are still unable to control how we relate to our technology, even just for a few days.

Such observations led us to thinking that perhaps instead of trying to turn away from tech in order to understand our minds, we should be turning toward it and using our digital habits as a mirror to understand our mental habits. The inescapable and mundane moments of Zooming, doomscrolling and emailing could then be used to deepen our grasp on how the mind works! This was the beginning of our friendship and work together in Mind over Tech.

We began to research the relationship between the mind and technology more deeply. We spoke to neuroscientists and behavioral psychologists, philosophers and AI experts as well as people designing digital interfaces. We've since developed programs for graduates, leaders and teams to help them take control of their tech use and over the years have trained thousands of professionals from companies such as Google, Vodafone and Deloitte. And we keep coming back to this idea of inner freedom: We should be able to choose when and how to engage with devices to support our goals, whether it is productivity, creativity or connection. And we should foster habits that help us facilitate that choice.

3. We Don't Pretend We're Perfect

You may assume that—as experts in this field—we now have a perfect relationship with tech. But, the reality of having a supercomputer on one's body at all times presents a real challenge to anyone. Every time there's an OS update, or we add another smart device to our home, or the secret algorithms curating our media feed are altered, our habits evolve and bring fresh challenges into our digital lives!

For this reason, anyone who promises a way to conquer all of tech's distractions and reach digital enlightenment is (we're sorry to say) deceiving you. More importantly, they are also missing the point. None of us can ever have a constantly perfect relationship with technology, for the same reason none of us can have the perfect life: We are all fundamentally bound by human limitations. But this is not something to despair over, because static perfection is not the goal. The best we can aspire to for ourselves, and for you, is an awareness of how we use our tech, always trying to align our digital habits with what's most important to us in that moment. A moment when we should feel awake and alive. We don't get to choose whether we live in a digital world or not, but we do get to choose *how* we engage with it. The continuous dance of working with your limitations to live your best digital life is one that will ultimately fill it with satisfaction and purpose.

And that dance begins with Part 1.

PART 1 Principles

The following three principles must be understood
in order to live your best digital life.
Trying to change your digital habits without
understanding them will severely limit
your long-term success.

Digital Tech Is an Extension of Your Mind

Or, How to Be a Better Cyborg

You may have heard the story of Officer Alex Murphy, a Detroit police officer who was tragically and brutally attacked in the line of duty. Officer Murphy was immediately rushed to the ER, where doctors worked tirelessly to try to revive him. After many hours, it became clear he wouldn't pull through without unprecedented intervention, which was—controversially—given the go-ahead. Doctors amputated his limbs and installed pioneering prosthetics in their place.

Murphy eventually made a full recovery, but the prosthetics changed him. Actuators in his new hands gave him enhanced strength sufficient to exert roughly 400 pounds of force—enough to lift the front of the average car over his head with one arm—and ocular implants allowed him to use a grid system to evaluate an environment for threats and calculate complex bullet trajectories in real-time. These tools made Murphy into the ultimate weapon against crime. They also nearly cost him his humanity. As you may have guessed by now, Officer Murphy is the protagonist of the 1987 movie *RoboCop*, and he is a cyborg.

You're (Probably) Not a Cyborg

It's probably safe to say you're not a cyborg, but to know for sure, let's analyze the word itself. A combination of cybernetic (the science of automated control systems) and organism, the term cyborg was originally coined by Manfred Clynes in the 1960s as he wrote about the emerging use of space suits enabling us to inhabit environments that lacked an atmosphere. One of the clearest definitions we've found describes a cyborg as "an organism that has restored function or extended abilities due to the integration of some artificial component or technology."

And yet, as Nicholas Carr wrote in his seminal 2010 book *The Shallows*, all technology—from the earliest tools of mankind to those of the future—can be understood as anything that extends our natural human abilities. Carr explains how all technology can be grouped into one of four broad categories, according to which of our abilities they extend. These categories are, in our words:

- Physical Strength (e.g., hammer, gun)
- Sensory Perception (e.g., radar, binoculars)
- Shaping Nature (e.g., dam, contraceptive pill)
- Mental Powers (e.g., calculator, typewriter)

Considered in this way, all technology enhances our natural abilities, and even something as humble as the coffee mug (extending our ability to hold piping hot, life-giving liquid) brings us a little closer to the cyborg camp. If that's true for tools as basic as a mug or a shovel, consider how much of an impact the more advanced digital technologies we all seem to engage with every day have on the very core of our humanity. For the last decade, the biggest companies in the world have been digital technology companies, and it's no exaggeration to say their products and services are transforming the way we live. More than that, much like the tools fused with

RoboCop's body, they are transforming who we are.

The digital technologies created by companies such as Apple, Google, Meta, Microsoft and more can be grouped into the last category: providing enhanced mental powers. Consider the following examples:

- Our smartphones can feed us nearly any aspect of humanity's knowledge and history within a few seconds.
- Generative AI reads 100-page documents in seconds and summarizes their key points. It can also compose spontaneous works of fiction in various styles.
- Neural networks can spot patterns in human language and behavior and draw remarkable insights and predictions about what we might say or do next.
- Augmented reality headsets do the hard work of visualizing complex data and ideas in our field of view without us needing to break a sweat.

Each of these technologies allows us to perform feats beyond our native mental capacities, making it possible to think deeper, faster and with far less effort. This is why Steve Jobs famously described the computer as "a bicycle for our minds." But just because we're all using tech that makes it easier for us to think or communicate that doesn't make us all cyborgs, surely? Technology is still separate from our physical form. Right?

And yet, there's an undeniable attachment. Consider the last time you accidentally left your smartphone in another room. How long do you need to be separate from your phone before you start to feel a little vulnerable, like something is missing? How many seconds does it take you to start looking for the Wi-Fi details whenever you arrive at a new location? How do your spelling abilities hold up to those of your school days if you don't have access to spell-check? We often don't quite feel fully "ourselves" without our devices. Still, it's not like we've got stuff implanted in our brains or attached to our eyes. Right?

Well—not for long. Telepathy—the evocatively named computer-brain interface created by Neuralink—is just one example of technology that has successfully integrated its first unit with a human body. Neuralink's product is already quite small (the size of a coin) and is embedded flush within your skull, with a series of 64 threads (considerably thinner than strands of hair) inserted into your brain to record neural activity. Noland Arbaugh, the first human to receive the implant, was playing various video games with only his mind as the controller just weeks after his surgery. Neuralink's ultimate goal is to achieve a symbiosis between the biological mind and the digital mind, allowing users to directly interface with current and future AI technologies with little more than a thought.

You may be thinking, "Well, I would never get one of those weird brain implants," but at some point—who's to say just how soon—it may not be such an easy choice. When over 77 percent of the U.S. population owns a smartphone, choosing not to have one is possible, but it's also deeply inconvenient and arguably puts you at a considerable disadvantage in numerous situations. Once a certain number of people decide "a weird brain implant" isn't all that weird, or (more likely) is a price worth paying for a new level of easy, frictionless living, you'll find yourself wondering if you want to be one of the only people without one. You may not even have a choice if your government, employer or insurance provider requires it. What's more, you may not even feel a shift happening. After all, we all woke up one day to find ourselves constantly lost in our phones. But this didn't happen overnight. We slowly slid into this situation without noticing.

Whether or not you choose to think of yourself as a cyborg is irrelevant. What's key to understand here is that whether you like it or not, the digital technology you use today is a direct extension of your mind—and therefore an intimate part of your very existence. Put another way, if you want to examine your relationship with technology, you must simultaneously look intimately at your own mind.

What We Mean by "Mind"

Since we'll be using the word "mind" quite a bit over the course of this book, and because the meaning of the word has been philosophically debated for millennia, we want to clarify what it means to us, and how we'll be using it.

If we look closely at how we talk about human minds in everyday conversation, we usually describe them as if they are advanced bits of tech—biological computers of sorts. This is unsurprising. Throughout history, humans have consistently used the latest emerging technologies as a metaphor to help explain or illustrate our intelligence. As artificial intelligence expert George Zarkadakis points out in his book *Our Own Image*, the invention of hydraulic engineering in the 3rd century B.C. popularized the idea of different fluids in the body (the "humors") that were believed to account for both our physical and mental functions. By the 1500s, gadgets driven by springs and gears inspired leading thinkers such as René Descartes to conclude that humans are complex machines. Similarly, by the mid-1800s, inspired by advances in networking communications, the German physicist Hermann von Helmholtz compared the brain to a telegraph.

Continuing this trend, the prevailing metaphor that we use today to understand human intelligence is that of computers and smartphones. Our language reflects this, with phrases like "Let me give you the download," "I need to recharge my batteries" and "Do you have the bandwidth for this?" being commonplace. Even the term "multitasking" is borrowed from computer processes. As a result of this framing, we tend to discuss the mind purely in terms of inputs (i.e., the things we see, hear, think, feel) and outputs (i.e., the things we say, write or type) and disregard all that complex, hard to explain stuff happening in between.

So if the mind is not merely a computer, what is it? Most people tend to think of the mind as being in the head. Physically, this is where the brain is, and this is where neurologists can see all our mental processes happening: things like seeing, remembering, forgetting, feeling and dreaming. While many neuroscientists and philosophers credit the neurons in the brain with being solely responsible for every experience you might have, just as many disagree. They argue that the mind is something non-physical—that, while it may relate to our brains somehow, ultimately it exists beyond them. We aren't attempting to solve this age-old debate within these pages, but we want to emphasize that when we use the term "mind" throughout the book, we mean "that which contains all of your subjective experience."

For example, imagine you stub your toe on a door and start shouting in pain: There is a "body" aspect to this experience (objective) and a "mind" aspect to it—a perception of discomfort that will be different depending on how resilient or sensitive you are (subjective). The second aspect of this experience is, to us, the work of the mind. In this book, whenever we refer to your mind, we're referring to your subjective experience. We are talking about your conscious awareness of being here right now: touching, thinking, feeling, all of it.

In sum, we don't consider the mind to be the same thing as a computer-brain physical entity. It is not separate from the physical body, but it is also not limited to neural activity. "Mind" is the whole embodied experience of being engaged with the world around us—of being a person.

If pervasive digital technologies are an extension of our

minds, then our smartphones, for example, are an extension of our embodied subjective experience of life itself. This is why "digital life" is such an apt phrase and why understanding how to live your best digital life involves much more than simply putting your phone in a drawer for a few hours or reaching inbox zero. It is not simply about reducing the negative impact of tech and being less distracted. To thrive in digital environments, we need to roll up our sleeves and start working with our minds. In order to do this, we'll first need to dive into insights from numerous disciplines—from neuroscience and psychology to philosophy and mindfulness.

Going Beyond the Digital Detox

How do most approaches to improving your life with tech begin? Maybe you've been told to simply take time away from your phone. Try a digital detox or a weekly digital "sabbath." Digital well-being strategies like these are usually about making sure that technology is not a harmful force in your life. The underlying premise behind these recommendations is that "too much" technology is bad for us, so all we have to do is reduce and limit our use of it and voilà! While there's merit to moderation, there's a better way. We don't just want to limit our tech use to ensure we don't get stressed, anxious, exhausted and depressed—we want to leverage and embrace technology in ways that positively enhance our well-being. That's our dream for ourselves and for you, and the premise of this book. Digital well-being, when considered in this way, is about developing the mindsets and skills for a healthy, positive relationship with our tech.

Our focus on the positive potential of digital habits is inspired by the work of Martin Seligman. When he was a young psychologist, he, like most of his peers, believed overcoming negative conditions (depression, anxiety and other mental health issues) would be enough to make people happy. But in his research, he found the most he could achieve by removing negative conditions was to "bring people back to zero." Sure, they weren't suffering as much, but they weren't thriving either. In other words, he discovered that gaining happiness and removing misery are different things, requiring different skills. When Seligman became president of the American Psychological Association in 1998, he used his inaugural speech to consolidate a new paradigm in psychology. Instead of focusing on mental illness and pathology alone, he advocated for scientists to study what is good and positive in life, a field now known as positive psychology. The scientific community heeded his call to action, and today, there are many theories and research programs focused on examining the things that make life more enjoyable and exploring how to define, quantify and create a positive sense of well-being.

In 2012, Seligman reviewed all the research and created a model that maps out the key pillars of well-being. There are six components in total (with the last being added by researchers building from Seligman's work), forming the acronym PERMAH:

Positive emotions
Engagement
Relationships
Meaning
Accomplishments
Health

At first glance, this might seem obvious ("That couldn't possibly have taken years and myriad grants to sort out..."). What makes these six components distinct, though, is that humans have been found to pursue them for their own sake rather than as a means to an end. We don't pursue relationships for the sake of meaning, or health for the sake of positive emotions—each is important to us for its own reasons. In addition, despite being interconnected, these six components of well-being can be defined and measured independently of one another (every researcher's dream!). Together, they provide a powerful framework for understanding happiness. If you can identify the skills required to increase your experience of these components, then you have a direct means to create a better life for yourself.

Taking this framework and applying it to our digital lives— if we can identify the set of skills that's required to increase our experience of these six components while interacting with technology—then we can create a better digital life for ourselves. Seligman himself is optimistic about the role technology plays in improving our well-being, saying in a TED talk that technology can help us "increase the amount of tonnage of human happiness on the planet."

We believe it's possible to embrace technology fully and also increase your well-being. If we think of digital tech as an extension of our minds, then this makes sense—when used intentionally, our smartphones have the potential to extend our experiences of happiness and of human flourishing itself.

The problem is that we often experience the opposite— our digital devices frequently leave us distracted, distressed and disconnected. But don't let this discourage you. In Part 2 of this book, we'll introduce a methodology to not only limit these negative conditions in our digital lives but also confidently explore ways of embracing technology that enhance the various components of human flourishing. In Part 3, we'll guide you in applying this methodology to each of the six components of PERMAH, devoting a chapter to each, in order to start living your best digital life in a very practical way.

Your Tech Choices Matter

Have you ever felt that the more you rely on GPS, the harder it is to navigate without it? A 2020 study showed that frequent GPS users exhibited a decline in spatial memory. Thanks to the neuroplasticity of our brains (meaning that they are constantly rewiring themselves—right up to the day we die!), the more we use any technology, the more our brains adapt to using it. But these changes in our brains aren't always negative. For example, people who play a lot of action-oriented video games have been shown to improve their ability to track multiple objects in a fast-moving environment. When we talk about technology as an extension of our natural human capacities, it sounds as though these capacities are fixed. In reality, we are constantly evolving and adapting to the tools we use.

Many people, especially in the tech industry, frame technology as simply a tool we can pick up and use when it helps us—a view known as tech instrumentalism. Others argue technology influences us so fundamentally that it shapes who we are and what we want in the first place—a view known as tech determinism. For any tech, it turns out both views are true. Take a ubiquitous piece of technology such as the car. On one hand, it's just a tool, sitting patiently in the driveway until we need it. However, if we think of this technology as being more influential, we might argue that having a car begins to change us. Going to the store suddenly becomes a lot easier, and as a result, we begin to spend more money while also exercising less. It also begins to change the way we relate to the environment around us—what was once a quaint country road that we enjoyed walking down is now a pothole-riddled nuisance that needs to be paved. Tech shapes who we are as a person—what we are capable of, and by extension, what we desire.

When she was a teenager, Menka was really excited to get her first satellite-connected compass as a gift ahead of an expedition with her friends. In general, Menka considered herself someone with a bad sense of direction, but having this compass gave her so much confidence that an hour into the journey, she felt comfortable suggesting a shortcut. By taking this less trodden path, her group ended up getting viciously chased by goats, but that's not the point! Simply having this small bit of technology in her pocket influenced her sense of identity and changed her behavior. Even today, Menka is confident with directions—provided she has her smartphone and there aren't any goats around.

When new technology changes what is possible, it changes culture. Philosopher Marshall McLuhan is credited with saying that we shape our tools, then our tools shape us. The advent of printed books encouraged the organization of knowledge to fit a linear process of reading, whereas the invention of radio furthered the oral tradition of storytelling. The internet encourages information-gathering while also encouraging (and requiring) a rapid shifting of focus. Describing the role of tech in our lives only in terms of extending our human capacities sells it short—the tools we use change the norms of our societies.

When it comes to putting in the effort to live our best digital lives, if you understand that technology influences who you are over time, then you will be a lot more careful about the details of your digital habits. Decisions you make about what tech to use (and how you use it) have consequences that reach beyond a particular moment in time. For example, choosing to capture your thoughts in a physical notepad instead of the Notes app on your phone could be a good way to avoid unnecessary distractions in the moment. But over time, it can also create the conditions for you to capture completely different types of insight only made possible with pen and paper—it will help you think in a different way. That's not to say it's better but that the choice you make matters and whatever you choose should be aligned with your goals. You should also be aware that the choices you make—especially with regard to new technology—can have unintended consequences, which is why choosing to use them mindfully is so important.

Your Best Digital Life Starts With You

A study conducted in California found that children who spent just five days without access to screens were better at reading emotions than their peers who had regular access to phones, computers and TVs. A 2021 study of young adults who own a smartphone found that 68.1 percent report neck pain (a syndrome called text neck). The negative impacts of how we are currently using our digital tech are undeniable.

Of course, using any technology carries a degree of risk. Considering cars again, while they allow you to travel long distances, they also pose a real threat of injury or even death in an accident. For this reason, car manufacturers have an ethical and legal obligation to create a safe product, regulators must ensure that standards are met, local authorities need to keep roads well-lit and so on—there's a long list of people responsible for ensuring your safety, and that's all happening before you show up at the dealership.

While the same guardrails should be in place for all technologies, the reality is that ethical design and regulation are often sorely lacking when it comes to big tech. This can be because digital technologies develop so fast that it takes time for their impact to be understood and for the appropriate safeguards to be put in place. But it is also clear that many tech companies are putting profits ahead of safety and doing whatever they can to avoid taking responsibility for the negative impacts of their products.

Organizations such as the Center for Humane Technology are doing great work to help change this situation, identifying and communicating principles such as "When we invent a new technology, we uncover a new class of responsibility." Elsewhere, regulations are being passed to protect tech users—whether it's the "right to be forgotten" by search engines, improving content moderation on social media platforms or banning the use of deceptive designs that make it difficult for users to cancel payments.

We want to be really clear—in order for all of us to live our best digital lives, it's absolutely crucial for the tech industry and its regulators to take more responsibility in identifying harmful practices and mitigating their impact. However, while we wait for more regulations to be put into place, our brains and behaviors are changing. Furthermore, the next wave of disruptive digital technologies is always just around the corner, and those technologies will escape regulation for years until they're more widely understood. And by then, it may be too late to put the digital implants back in the box.

In any case, even if significant changes are made and the most optimistic levels of regulation are applied, it never will be enough to guarantee a perfect relationship with tech because—like any relationship—it's a two-way street, and we also have a part to play.

For these reasons, we believe each of us has a responsibility to ourselves to tackle the part of this relationship we can control—how to best use the technologies in our lives. One of the most important skills that anyone can learn right now is how to make wise choices about what technology we use and how we use it in order to live in today's world while also protecting our minds and the quality of life that we value.

Make a Long-Term Investment in Your Digital Habits

The good news is that since digital tech is all about our minds, this book's methods for managing our relationship with technology are timeless and will remain relevant long after we're using flying cars and robot butlers. But it should be clear to you by now that it's also not a passive one-and-done process. As we saw with the positive psychology research, simply keeping negativity at bay isn't the same thing as truly flourishing. In the same way, there's extra work to be done to live your best digital life, and that work is each person's responsibility.

Digital technology is an integral part of our lives, so its negative impacts cause no end of trouble for us. But out of adversity come great opportunity. We believe seeing your technology simply as something to be tamed is a limiting perspective. Seen from another angle—by becoming deeply curious about how tech shapes who we are—our digital devices become a constant invitation to get to know our own minds better, identify what we value most and ultimately deepen our understanding of what it means to be human. Or, if you like, what it means to be a cyborg.

Summary

- Tech extends our mental capacities. Therefore, to live our best digital lives, we must work with our minds.

- By "mind," we don't simply mean the brain; we also refer to our bodies and entire subjective experience.

- Simply eliminating the negative impacts of our digital habits is not enough; we must actively develop digital habits that enable us to flourish.

- The tools we use shape us individually and collectively, which is why our tech choices matter deeply.

Choose Your Conveniences Carefully

Or, When to Be Wisely Lazy

Amid a severe snowstorm in the winter of 1482, Johannes Trithemius, a young German scholar (who was fleeing family strife) chanced upon an abbey and took refuge there. Moved by the peaceful atmosphere and inspired by the monks' dedication to a life of education and self-development, Trithemius decided to take vows himself. He thrived in this environment and was elected abbot within the next year. Under his leadership, the abbey's library greatly expanded. Trithemius's tenure coincided with the early years of the printing revolution, sparked by the Gutenberg Press's introduction of movable type around 1440. It marked a significant period in the dissemination of information and ideas.

Despite his passion for education, however, Trithemius was not always in favor of printed books. It's safe to assume he would have been keen to acquire a copy of the Gutenberg Bible for the abbey's library, but we know he was also very wary of it. Specifically, he had reservations about the trade-off that a printed Bible represented. In the treatise "In Praise of Scribes," he reminds people that hand-scribing the Bible in beautiful illuminated letters was one of the major activities carried out by monks at the time. He explains the crucial role this laborious act plays in monks' spiritual development:

"As he is copying the approved texts he is gradually initiated into the divine mysteries...Every word we write is imprinted more forcefully on our minds since we have to take our time while writing and reading. The repeated reading of Scripture will inflame the mind of the writer."

Trithemius understood that there was deep value in the immense effort required to write and illustrate the book by hand. It involved pushing up against multiple limitations: the speed at which it could be written, the dexterity required to create the beautiful calligraphy and the knowledge needed to make the quills, ink and paper. By engaging their limitations in this way, the monks integrated all aspects of their minds and bodies in a process that facilitated a deeply embodied understanding of the text. To put it bluntly, it was an entirely different experience from buying a book.

It may seem hypocritical to pine for the days of hand-scribed tomes in a book that was written on a computer and edited via the internet. And yet, here we are. The printing press was undeniably a net positive, a remarkable piece of technology that changed our world in remarkable ways. But that doesn't mean Trithemius was wrong. With each new innovation, no matter how much easier it makes our lives or how it broadens our horizons, we also lose something. Taking stock of this each time we adopt the use of a new technology is an important step to ensure we use that tech mindfully. Otherwise, it's safe to say we won't know what we've lost until it's too late to get it back.

Humans Are
Fundamentally Limited

As humans, we share this fate of being fundamentally bound by our limitations. Our physical strength sets a limit on how fast we can run or how much weight we can carry. Each of our senses has a limitation—there are entire frequency ranges of sound and light that we'll never perceive. Our capacity for complex reasoning or regulating our emotions is limited by the size and structure of our brains, and our cognitive control means that we cannot perform two conscious tasks simultaneously (no matter how much we may believe the contrary). Our ability to harness and manipulate the natural world is also limited—we may be able to stimulate rain in a localized environment, but we can't control the macro weather patterns of Earth. We can even control birth rates—but ultimately, we can't control when we will die.

These limitations give rise to all kinds of challenges in everyday life. Thankfully for most of us (most of the time), these aren't life-threatening or serious hardships but rather different varieties of what we might describe as "inconveniences." It's having to get out of bed 20 minutes earlier to have enough time to scrape ice off the windshield before driving to work, having to spend several hours at a gym every week to stay in shape or having to pay close attention to the words and body language of those we wish to understand because we can't read minds (and in-person conversations sadly lack captions).

Pulling on the thread of any human limitation reveals an inconvenience, small or large. When we uncover these inconveniences, we have a choice: We can try to optimize our situation to minimize them, or we can (often grudgingly) try to accept the inconvenience for what it is. Most of us, when given the opportunity, will unfailingly choose the former. After all, why make life harder than it needs to be?

The Spectrum of Convenience

Printing a book is certainly easier than writing it by hand, but Johannes Trithemius was both for *and* against printing the Bible because he saw that the value of each option depends on the context. For ordinary folk, the convenience of having direct access to the text was invaluable. But for a monk, the same convenience potentially robbed him of a slower, engaging practice that deepened his faith.

Convenience is not objectively bad, but it doesn't always represent the better choice either—it depends. The ability to tap your phone a couple of times to conjure a hot, delicious meal can be an absolute lifesaver. But it's not a money saver. Equally, receiving messages from anyone, anywhere, anytime can give you vital information at just the right moment and help maintain friendships across continents, but it can also be an endless source of distraction and, counterintuitively, can even become the reason that you never see some friends face to face.

Given that the benefits of all the shiny technological conveniences that make our lives more efficient, optimized and comfortable are so easy to articulate (and aggressively marketed), it is hard to notice their subtle costs to us as human beings. Few of us spend much time considering what potential benefits could be hiding within an inconvenience, since we are too busy finding a solution to get rid of it. We're not suggesting that you ignore the more convenient option when there is one, only that doing so should be treated as an exchange, a trade-off. When we acquire a new piece of tech, we have to give something up, too—there is always a subtle cost involved. To help identify this cost, we find it helpful to consider where any piece of technology may fall on a spectrum:

INCONVENIENCE ←----------------------→ **CONVENIENCE**

In any given situation, it's always possible to make something more or less convenient than it currently is—and depending on your perspective, each direction along the spectrum has its advantages. This allows you to ask the question, "What degree of convenience is best for me right now?" The answer will depend on multiple factors: What kind of a day are you having? What are your current priorities? How urgent is the situation? And, ultimately, what do you value most? There is no single right answer, nor is today's answer the same as one you might have a week, month or year from now. The point is to ask the question. And in many cases, big tech wants us to ignore this question altogether.

Despite the fact that finding the best spot on this spectrum is so personal and subjective, the way tech is designed means we generally default toward choosing more convenience. Even on the days when you know it would be better to walk to work and get some fresh air and clear your head, it's tempting to jump in the car. The very term "modern conveniences" has become a synonym for "modern technologies."

To help us live our best digital lives, we need an ongoing evaluation process for staying open to innovations without automatically deferring to every new degree of convenience available.

Your Inconvenience Is Someone Else's Best Practice

British journalist Oliver-James Campbell was only 15 years old when he was diagnosed with substantial hearing loss, which suddenly explained all the difficulties he had with specific sounds and noisy environments. As a result, he began to use hearing aids, but after some time, he stopped. The devices gave him access to sounds he was previously unaware of, and he found everyday noises like rustling grass or beeping appliances intolerable. The choice to opt out of using hearing aids came with complications and risks (including being attacked due to mishearing someone once in a late-night incident). But leaning into these inconveniences allows Campbell to live a life that he values. At his annual checkups, he still politely explains to his doctor that he prefers not to be assisted by the convenience of hearing aids.

By contrast, consider Neil Harbisson: a British artist based in New York who was born with achromatic vision. Harbisson can't see color—only black, white and shades of gray. Given artists' particular interest in colors and perception, Harbisson applied his creative mind to invent what he calls a "cyborg antenna"—a piece of tech with a camera on one end that was surgically implanted into his head. It allows him to "hear" colors through frequency vibrations in his skull (using the same bone conduction found in hearing aids). This doesn't just compensate for his color blindness—it has expanded his sensory world, and he can even perceive ultraviolet and infrared light. By leaning into the convenience this technology provided, Harbisson now has a unique perspective of the world that has only deepened his art practice.

These two stories illustrate just how personal the choice of where to position yourself on the spectrum of convenience can be. Campbell's story is a journey of rejecting the convenience of digital aids in favor of self-acceptance and independence, facing the world with the senses he was born with despite the challenges doing so might present. Harbisson's tale is one of embracing technological symbiosis not just to overcome a challenge, but to enhance and extend his sensory perception far beyond the natural human condition.

We all have different value systems as well as different needs from our technology. Ideally, each of us would go through a similar process of defining which tech-powered conveniences we consider to be a helpful aid versus an unhelpful alteration of our human experience. One person's inconvenience is another person's best digital life.

Our Low Tolerance for Inconvenience

No matter how much we'd like to live in a world free from the woes of inconvenience, it's simply not possible. This, of course, is not breaking news. Philosophers, sages and parents of deeply disappointed children with melted ice cream cones have long been patiently pointing out: Things will never be perfect.

When we reject this hard truth, however, we add salt to the wound. Imagine sitting in your car stuck in traffic, late for an appointment and getting mad at all the other drivers. There are two levels of suffering here—the basic inconvenience of being delayed by other cars and our frustration at the situation. While we can't control the traffic, we can control how we react to it, which could potentially save us a great deal of discomfort. But we often find ourselves getting wound up by the smallest things. Even when we know better, it's hard to accept ordinary inconveniences.

That's not to say our lives shouldn't be made more comfortable—this is why we have come to love and trust technology so much. Over the course of history, human ingenuity has created technology that has transformed our lives for the better. The modern toilet, for example, in use in homes since the 1880s, has saved roughly a billion lives by improving sanitation conditions! 3D printing, which started being used more widely in 2010, now saves many thousands of lives every year through the printing of prosthetics. Looking at these improvements cumulatively, technological advances in healthcare, medicine and hygiene have doubled human lifespans in just two centuries. At the beginning of the 19th century, the average life expectancy was less than 30 years, with no country achieving more than 40 years. In 2022, the United Nations estimated the global average of life expectancy to be over 71 years.

And yet, no matter how good our lives get, it can still be difficult to accept the smallest of everyday problems—the ache in your body after a tiring day at work, not being able to find your keys as you walk out the door, the seemingly endless final seconds before the microwave timer dings. Despite technology making just about everything easier, it seems that the more convenient our lives become, the less resilient we are to challenges. Like Hans Christian Andersen's tale "The Princess and the Pea," the smoother our lives, the more we notice the smallest of bumps.

Humans may have even evolved to notice inconveniences. An evolutionary hypothesis known as the negativity bias suggests we are more attuned and responsive to negative information because it's beneficial for our survival. In this way, every limitation we rub up against, no matter how small and inconsequential, is a nagging reminder of the ultimate limitation: the finite nature of our lives.

The Dream of a Frictionless Life

At the extreme end of this intolerance toward inconvenience, Google co-founder Sergey Brin claims he has no plans to die. He's part of a movement of the elite and superrich of Silicon Valley who are "solving" death. In a bizarre post on Twitter, one of these people, Ethereum co-founder Vitalik Buterin, wrote, "Aging is a humanitarian disaster that kills as many people as WW2 every two years." PayPal co-founder Peter Thiel has similarly lamented, "We should either conquer death or at least figure out why it's impossible."

What's interesting about this is that it reveals the underlying ethos deeply embedded in the tech industry: Every human limitation—even *death*—is merely an inconvenient problem to be solved. Of course, none of us want to die, but of the approximately 109 billion people who have ever lived, every single one of them has died. Many would argue that to remove death would strip life of its meaning. Whatever your position, if entrepreneurs aren't stopping to consider the potential trade-offs of removing something as inevitable as our own mortality, then they certainly aren't making nuanced decisions about the trade-offs related to the smaller limitations of life.

In recent years, as the pace and direction of technological progress have become increasingly shaped by the beliefs and actions of Silicon Valley, a particular way of relating to our problems has become dominant: design thinking. In this approach, product teams start observing and empathizing with a situation, then articulate what the problem at hand is in order to develop and refine ideas until a solution is found. Both of us writing this book have a background in design thinking and have lived and loved this approach to innovation for years—it has provided a welcome shift in philosophy for nearly every industry. The discipline to stay loyal to solving a problem throughout the creative process makes it much more likely that the end product delivered will serve actual needs, rather than assumed or imagined ones. As Steve Jobs said, "You've got to start with the customer experience and work backwards to the technology. You can't start with the technology and try to figure out where you're going to try to sell it." This keeps a company's focus on the customer, not just the tech.

But as with every approach, design thinking has its downsides. Designers can become obsessed with discovering customer problems to solve (their salary and their company's business success depend on discovering these problems too). And, as Warren Buffett's late business partner, Charlie Munger, famously taught: "Show me the incentives and I'll show you the outcome." Given that the tech industry is incentivized to find problems in our lives, problems will always be found. Or, to use tech industry lingo, if you look carefully enough, you will always find friction to reduce or pain points to resolve. And no matter how trivial a problem is, with enough creativity and a large marketing budget, it can become a problem worth paying to solve.

In many ways, today's cultural narratives conflate happiness and comfort as if they are the same thing. As a result, it doesn't take much to convince us to want a product that promises any kind of comfort—a solution to a problem we didn't know we had. Once you've seen one of those ice cream scoops that warms up when you hold it, making scooping quicker, easier and cleaner, you'll start seeing a problem where perhaps before you didn't. This may seem like a fairly benign example (and if you're about to look up this magical scoop, hold that thought), but each such problem solved feeds a dream of a completely frictionless life.

Sleepwalking Into Danger

Maybe all of this doesn't seem like a big deal to you. So what if you download a few unnecessary apps or buy a couple of things you didn't really need? Hasn't advertising been pulling this trick on us for decades?

Yes. But it's important to understand what's at stake here. Individually, none of these conveniences matter, but each of them has the impact of subtly resetting our expectations for life, reducing our capacity to tolerate inconvenience. The culture we live in has become increasingly greased toward convenience, a fact that bleeds into our decision-making. Over time, the more convenient option becomes our default. "Whatever's closer." "Whichever place delivers."

We stop making choices intentionally and instead engage autopilot. The more we let our unconscious habits inform our choices, the more mind-numbing our lives become and the less capable we are of thinking for ourselves and working out what's best for us. What we need to thrive may not always be more convenient.

In the 2008 Pixar film *WALL-E*, humanity has quit Earth to live on a spaceship called the *Axiom*, where life is comfortable and overwhelmingly convenient. People live in floating La-Z-Boy chairs that take them wherever they like and provide them with all the food and entertainment they could ever want. In the 700 years humanity has lived in space, it hasn't occurred to anyone that another form of existence is possible, and it's easy to see why. But as the story develops, we see that perhaps some of the "problems" solved by their technologically advanced lifestyles aren't problems at all. In one of the final scenes, a robot explains to the captain that the spaceship is the safest place to ensure survival rather than returning to live on Earth. Finally, the frustrated captain replies, "I don't want to survive. I want to live!" He has come to realize that an entirely frictionless life isn't the best one for him.

The movie goes on to show how, upon their arrival on terra firma, the humans have to re-learn basic skills like walking around and growing food. In Principle 1, we looked at how we don't simply shape our tools, but the tools we use consistently shape us. If the majority of our everyday tools are geared toward convenience, how might this be shaping us? What skills will atrophy without us realizing?

Making Discerning Choices Is an Art

How do we avoid ending up like the captain from *WALL-E*, suddenly waking up to the fact that our overreliance on convenience has robbed our lives of meaning?

We've already looked at two examples of people living deliberately, the artist who can hear colors and the journalist who chooses not to wear a hearing aid, but these are extreme examples where the choice is either all-in or all-out. It is interesting (and perhaps more useful) to also consider examples where decisions are made more discerningly on a case-by-case basis.

Take photographer and filmmaker Martijn Doolaard, who, in 2021, bought two dilapidated cabins in Italy and began renovating them to create an off-grid homestead. Doolaard is exploring the benefits of living a deliberately inconvenient life. Yet, he hasn't rejected technology. Far from it. He uses a sophisticated drone, camera and laptop to create beautiful footage of his everyday experiences and regularly uploads them to YouTube (where he also gets tips and encouragement from more than 700K subscribers). It's apparent that Doolaard chooses each piece of tech on an individual basis, depending on how it supports his underlying values.

This example shows that in order to make discerning choices in all areas of your digital life, it helps to have clarity about your goals and values and a reliable way of assessing your digital habits in light of them. This is easier said than done, and it takes time to develop the clarity and skills to do this well.

Use Your Values to Choose Your Conveniences

Seeing others be discerning about the tech they bring into their lives can be inspiring. But it can be difficult to find that same clarity for ourselves. How can you know which "conveniences" you should choose or avoid?

Try this exercise: Draw a spectrum of convenience, then write the technology or digital habit you'd like to assess on a sticky note. In the upcoming example, we'll use the food delivery app Uber Eats. Consider where this falls on the spectrum of convenience for you at this moment in time (remember, your answers are subject to change). In the image below, two individuals have done this exercise:

- The yellow sticky note was placed by a financially secure individual, for whom ordering food through Uber Eats is nothing but a huge convenience.
- The orange sticky note was placed by a less financially secure individual. Uber Eats is still convenient, but it's also pricey, making it less convenient.

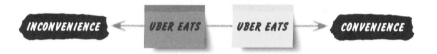

Once you have mapped the technology onto the spectrum of convenience, add another axis representing the extent to which the technology supports or undermines a value that is important to you. **We call this the Values Exercise.**

In the previous example, the person who used the yellow sticky note is on a strict weight loss program, so even though it is much more convenient for them to order food at the end of a long day, it undermines their values around health and is therefore an unhelpful convenience. On the other hand, the person who used the orange sticky note rarely gets to see their partner (who works nights), so ordering food to free up some precious quality time together supports their values.

Values Exercise

In some instances, your values may be very clear to you; in others, they won't. Don't worry if they are not clear—this is your invitation to reflect on what you value most in any given context. Looking into your relationship with tech can deepen your understanding of what really matters to you and ultimately who you are as a person. Remember, no two people will consistently complete this exercise the same way.

Choosing some conveniences and rejecting others based on your values can be challenging work. But hopefully, you've seen by now that some friction can be good for us. Like Trithemius's monks scribing texts, occasionally doing things the harder way is more fulfilling, and we'll explore examples of what this looks like in our modern digital lives throughout the book.

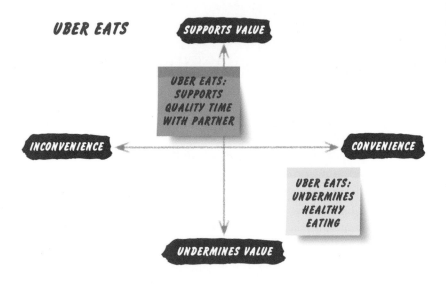

Summary

- Human limitations give rise to inconveniences, which we experience as friction—things feel harder, effortful and deliberate.

- While technology offers conveniences to overcome almost every limitation, there is often value in embracing them instead.

- Knowing when to choose convenience or inconvenience is a deeply personal process, but it is also a skill that can be learned.

- It all comes down to values and what is meaningful for us. If we don't think about this, then it is far too easy to default to the conveniences marketed to us.

- Practice evaluating whether conveniences are meaningfully helpful or not using the Values Exercise.

Digital Habits Can Be Tamed With Intention

Or, How to Wake a Digital Zombie

Every day when Jonathan comes home, he hangs his keys on a hook by the door—a useful habit that's developed over the years so he always knows where to find them. Recently, however, when he got home he was startled by the sound of his keys smashing on the floor. What just happened? In that moment, he realized he'd forgotten to put the hook back after painting the hallway. He had unconsciously acted in a way that no longer suited the situation he was in. The result may have looked like a slapstick gag from a Buster Keaton film, but it illustrates an important note about our habits: Automating your behavior is only useful to a point, and when habits become entirely unconscious, things can easily go wrong.

Habits Automate Your Behavior

Our lives are full of habits: getting dressed, brushing your teeth, checking the sports scores. Most of these behaviors sound pretty mundane when we list them, but that's kind of the point—they are things we do multiple times every day, and we need ways to do them consistently while using the smallest amount of brainpower possible. Habits are powerful because they promise to make good behavior second nature. You can think of habits as being similar to an algorithm. They are automated routines that, once started, follow the same patterns of behavior again and again. As soon as you begin unscrewing the cap on your toothpaste, the routine takes over, and without needing to think about it, a clean set of teeth is all but inevitable. How many times have you stopped brushing your teeth halfway through and forgotten to continue? Probably not many.

This ability to automate behavior is powerful. We quickly learn to navigate complexity in our lives by relying on routines to do the heavy lifting for us. As long as our habits serve our needs, they allow us to pursue the life we want more efficiently, without having to think about what we're doing all that often. Of course, we're only human—inevitably, we end up automating some behaviors that don't serve us as well. But overall, as long as we are able to accumulate more habits that benefit us than those that don't, our routines give us a healthy sense of control over our lives.

In order to live your best digital life, it's crucial to cultivate digital habits that serve you well. Yet, as you may well have discovered, this is incredibly difficult to do. You may have success establishing habits in the less digital parts of your life—such as your morning run, your daily commute or the way you set up your coffee maker the night before so you don't have to do so first thing in the morning when you're still rubbing the sleep out of your eyes—and yet you still find it difficult to get any of your desired digital habits to stick. If so, you are not alone. But what's going on here? Why is it so difficult to stay in control of our actions when using our digital devices? To answer that, let's dive into the science of how habits work.

How Habits Work

However simple or complex a habit is, all automated behavior is learned through the repetition of four universal steps:

1. **Context** Your underlying need(s) in your current situation
2. **Belief** Confidence that a particular action will satisfy your need(s)
3. **Response** Performing that action to achieve the desired results
4. **Reward** Your brain giving you satisfaction and feedback to reinforce your correct belief

Moving through these four steps again and again forms a habit loop. The first time you engage in a soon-to-be habit, your behavior is highly deliberate and effortful, but the reward creates the conditions for the same behavior to play out more easily the next time. As it's repeated again and again, the behavior becomes more familiar until eventually, you start doing it with very little thought and effort. For example, consider the first time you try something new, like drinking coffee:

1. **Context** You wake up in the morning and want to feel more awake
2. **Belief** Other people drink coffee to wake up, so perhaps that will work for you
3. **Response** You go out and buy yourself a coffee
4. **Reward** It tastes funny, but you notice you feel perkier

Everything takes a lot of effort here—your belief is not that strong, and you need to consciously make the decision to try coffee. You need to go somewhere new and navigate the coffee menu to figure out what a single-shot macchiato is. It doesn't immediately taste great, but overall, you do feel like it helped make you more alert. Your brain acknowledges this by releasing chemicals, including the neurotransmitter dopamine. At this stage, there's no guarantee you will start habitually drinking coffee—depending on many factors, it can take anywhere between 18 to 254 days of repeated behavior for things to become fully automatic. But your interest is piqued. Perhaps you'll try it again.

Each morning that you have a coffee and repeat these four steps, the Reward you receive (dopamine) creates a stronger motivation to repeat the process. With every repetition, the routine becomes increasingly automatic. Dopamine increases our motivation to act and therefore drives the loop. Each time we reach the Reward phase, a chemical is released that makes us feel good. Crucially, however, dopamine also plays a big role in the Belief phase. Research has shown that up to 10 times the amount of dopamine is released in *anticipation* of a reward than from the reward itself. This is what creates the strong craving to have a coffee once the habit is well established. At this point, the habit loop looks like this:

1. **Context** You wake up in the morning and want to feel more awake
2. **Belief** "I'm someone who needs coffee to feel more awake. I need one now."
3. **Response** You press a button on your coffee machine to make your favorite coffee
4. **Reward** You feel human again. Is it too soon to have another coffee?

Understanding how the four steps of the habit loop work can help you shape your behavior. If you want to build a specific habit, engage with each step in the loop and ensure it can be easily repeated. The opposite is also true: To break a habit, make each step in the loop harder to accomplish. To return to our original example, it'll be easier to cut down on your daily coffee intake if you get rid of your coffee maker. Think that sounds insane? Now imagine that your coffee maker is your phone.

Digital Habits Are Difficult to Tame

Sadly, the moment we unlock our phones or open our laptops, there's no telling what we will do next. We may have engaged our technology with a specific goal (e.g., reply to a message), but we could end up doing any number of things (e.g., checking the weather, watching a video, sharing that video with a friend, deleting some junk mail, learning about a coupon from a mailing list you subscribed to 10 years ago that expires in an hour, trying to find a use for the coupon before accepting that you don't dress like that anymore, seeing what the gang from college is up to, realizing it's Greta's kid's birthday tomorrow, looking at photos of that kid from just a year ago while you wonder where the time goes, coming to grips with your own mortality as you seek out another meme to express how you're feeling in this instant so you can share that feeling with the world or at least your spouse and so on).

This routine isn't just exhausting, it's disorienting. Imagine if every time you started to brush your teeth, you instantly became sidetracked by a hundred different activities. You'd never brush your teeth—and would likely feel as if you were losing your mind. But this helter-skelter, wholly distracted experience is pretty much the routine as far as our digital hygiene is concerned. Even worse, unlike our dental hygiene routines, we pick up our phones a lot more than twice a day. In fact, a study by the research firm dscout tracked the phone usage of 94 Android owners over five days and found that the average user touches their phone 2,617 times per day. That's a lot of opportunities for distraction and for our habits to stray off course.

Since you are reading this book, it's likely you have already tried several different strategies to improve your relationship with tech. Maybe you've tried limiting the number of times you mindlessly reach for your phone by putting it in a drawer. Or maybe you've tried improving your sleep by charging your phone away from your bed. Perhaps you've tried to reduce your anxiety by deleting your go-to doomscrolling apps from your device. Whatever the case, if you are anything like us, you'll have found it hard to turn these conscious interventions in your digital life into effective habits that work for you over the long term.

To make sense of why this is so difficult, we've identified five reasons your digital habits in particular are so difficult to tame. Since your mind is intimately involved in habit formation (and since technology is an extension of your mind), it won't be a surprise that many of these reasons relate to the psychological consequences of using digital tech.

1. Your Attention Is Scattered

Forming new digital habits requires your undivided attention. First, you must have the self-awareness to notice any underlying needs that could benefit from a new automated behavior (e.g., "I really need to stop checking my email every few minutes"). Then you must define the desired actions you'd like to automate (e.g., only check email in scheduled blocks of time). Next, you must diligently repeat the behavior at the right time in order to establish the habit (e.g., notice your finger as it extends toward the inbox button while you're at the supermarket and stop yourself from taking a quick peek). Finally, you must keep an eye on your actions over time and assess whether the new habit has managed to take root. All this requires you to not only be mindful of the details of your present actions but also to hold a broad level of awareness to ensure you're on the right track over time.

That's a lot to pay attention to, a problem that's exacerbated by the fact that our digital lives are absolutely full of distractions. Between the many communication channels, endless notifications, multiple screens and infinite sources of information, our limited attention is not just pushed to its capacity, it's actually diminishing. In the book *Attention Span*, Gloria Mark writes that the average time we hold our attention on a screen before switching to another has dropped from two and a half minutes in 2004 down to around 40 seconds in 2022. As a result of this fractured attention, establishing desired digital habits through the repetition of your intended actions is increasingly difficult.

2. Your Digital Habits Serve Someone Else's Agenda

The fact that your attention span is getting shorter shouldn't be a surprise. Documentaries like *The Social Dilemma* have made it very clear that the reason many digital products are offered for free is that their makers are in the business of capturing your attention. For most of us, encountering an ad while scrolling on Instagram, reading an article or watching a video is utterly mundane. Yet, behind these moments lies a $500 billion marketplace where our attention is continuously traded in split-second transactions. Online advertising drives the economy of the internet, and our attention is its fuel.

How do these companies keep your attention locked in like this? By designing products and services that create very habitual behavior. The book *Hooked* by Nir Eyal is considered a bible in Silicon Valley because it popularized a formula that exploits the habit loop based on psychologist B.F. Skinner's research from the 1940s. This research showed that when an action is repeated over time and can be engineered so that it creates an inconsistent reward (sometimes we are rewarded for performing it, sometimes not), then it creates very compulsive behavior. This originally led to the design of gambling machines where you press the same button again and again, sometimes receiving a reward, sometimes not—and today, it informs the design of many addictive apps and user interfaces.

Many other psychological tricks shape our digital behavior, and it's not just big tech firms that are deploying them. Content creators on platforms like YouTube and TikTok also rely on people regularly watching their videos for as long as possible, so they pursue strategies that ensure this result: posting videos at the same time each week, designing clickbait images and titles for their videos and editing their content with quick cuts and colorful, animated subtitles to hold your attention.

As a result, almost all of the interactions in your digital life have been carefully designed to cultivate habits in you that serve someone else's agenda. No wonder it feels like you're not really in control.

3. Digital Contexts Are Disorienting

Every behavior begins with a context—a combination of your underlying needs and the environment around you. At any given moment, you'll have multiple needs and desires (e.g., to curb your current hunger pangs, to eat *healthy*, to focus on creating your presentation, to reply to that urgent client email), but you don't act on all of them. While you may like to think you have control over which desires you choose to follow through on, the truth is that your environment often plays a more significant role in prompting your behavior. You may, for instance, insist that you will not snack between meals—until you encounter those chips left out on the counter. The good news is you can design your environments to set yourself up for success (e.g., keeping the chips out of sight).

Given that your context is the springboard that prompts you to take action, you also begin to associate habits with entire situations—exercising with going to the gym, working with being at the office and so on. But in our digital lives, these useful contextual prompts are often undermined because your devices present themselves as one giant, amorphous context that never really changes. What's worse, they often interfere with other contexts. Your devices are always present— even though you may be physically at the gym, the presence of your smartphone can dilute this context and distract from your workout. You could travel halfway around the world to a completely new culture but still find yourself in the same place—stuck on the same device, engaging in the same apps that define your digital bubble.

At the same time, the environment inside your devices is highly fluid and dynamic, constantly switching between endless tabs, incoming messages, app notifications and whatever else you have going on. This creates one big digital soup and often leaves you contextually bewildered—for example, opening your device to schedule an important work meeting only to then wind up getting bogged down in a heated family WhatsApp conversation.

Most of us have, at one point or another, been described as "always on our phones." But increasingly, we are in them— immersed in the whirlwind of contexts they create and unable to tame our digital habits as a result.

4. Your Beliefs Are Deeply Influenced in Digital Spaces

Research into habit change has uncovered something really helpful: Rather than relying on willpower, it's much easier to change your habits if you change your beliefs. Let's say you are trying to eat healthier. Rather than deploying your willpower to ignore the delicious smells wafting from the bakery you're trying to stride past with determination, if you pause and remind yourself that you are a healthy person (and that healthy people sometimes sacrifice short-term pleasure for long-term happiness), this will give you a far better chance at walking past without purchasing a cupcake.

Another way to look at this insight is that identity—which is made up of your beliefs about who you are and what you value in your life—is the most powerful way to affect long-term habit change. In his book *Atomic Habits*, James Clear explains, "Becoming the best version of yourself requires you to continuously edit your beliefs, and to upgrade and expand your identity."

The problem is that in the digital environment, it can be hard to know who you are. The experience of being online is constantly influencing your beliefs and identity—often without us noticing. Whether it's the Amazon algorithm recommending a pair of slippers it thinks you'll love or an influencer you follow on social media raving about a new magic powder for green juice, it can be hard to discern whether we buy into something (a product, service or even a whole ideology) based on our own experiences and insights or we are being overly influenced by the digital spaces we inhabit.

Even something as simple as a 5-star rating makes us believe that a product is superior to that of a similar one with 4.5 stars, despite knowing that many of the reviews are intentionally manipulative (a recent study that examined 33.5 million reviews for bestselling products on Amazon found that 43 percent were unreliable). It's hard to shake off these carefully designed and heavily invested in digital nudges and instead think for ourselves.

5. Digital Habits Get Stuck on Autopilot

At first, building habits to automate the things that work well for us so that we don't have to think about it anymore sounds great. But there's a flip side: If we become too reliant on the unconscious nature of our habits, we can end up blindly following routines that no longer serve us.

This may not be such a huge problem in your non-digital life (thinking back to our opening story—Jonathan rarely redecorates, so his keys-on-the-floor incident is a one-off), but it can cause havoc in your digital life where behavior is on autopilot but the context changes all the time. Checking your email at your desk, in the office restroom and at your kid's party are three very different contexts. The habits that serve you in one of those environments will not necessarily do so in another—and when those habits are unconscious, it's easy for them to play out at the wrong moment. How many times have you quickly checked your work email on a weekend or while on vacation, purely out of habit? Or found yourself unintentionally scrolling through your social media feeds while in the middle of writing a work email?

If you only realize you are doing these things *after* they have happened, then your actions are entirely unconscious and are likely causing as much harm as they are doing you good.

There's No Such Thing as a Bad Digital Habit

Given everything we've just explored, you may be feeling a little overwhelmed. It can feel as though taming your digital habits is nearly impossible and that you are forever doomed to be beholden to your digital devices, locked into patterns of distraction and bad habits.

It's important to note that what everyone needs from technology is different. For that reason, we believe there is no such thing as a "bad" digital habit. When making healthy choices in our non-digital lives, there are certain habits, such as smoking, that are clinically bad. Everything about them is at odds with the goal of living a healthier life, no matter who you are. But in our digital lives, things are far less clear-cut. Endlessly scrolling through social media is a legitimate requirement for people working in marketing or customer relations. In these instances, the act of spending long periods on social platforms is therefore not inherently bad, since doing so puts a roof over your head. Yet at the same time, it is clearly not good for many people who find themselves uncontrollably locked in a scrolling session.

Instead of thinking about digital habits as good or bad, we prefer to consider whether or not they are *intentional*. Playing a lot of chess online? Great! Unless you are actually supposed to be finishing that essay due tomorrow, in which case the chess is unintentional. Watching *Seinfeld* on Netflix? Wonderful! But only if that's the initial reason you opened your laptop and not because that article on Earth, Wind & Fire led you down a rabbit hole that ended with revisiting Elaine's little kicks.

Framing your digital habits in this way is helpful because it invites you to take the judgment and self-critical thoughts out of the equation and instead focuses you on something far more pragmatic: Is your current digital behavior intentional? Ultimately, this is the only thing that really matters. By using this question as your guide, while holding awareness of all of the challenges that we've explored in this chapter, you will be best placed to begin unpicking the knot of your digital habits and living your best digital life.

Making Your Digital Habits Intentional

We're using the word "intentional" a lot here. Let's take a moment to unpack what this means. There are two defining characteristics that signal whether or not a digital habit is intentional:

1. The extent to which the behavior serves your goals and values
2. The extent to which you are aware of the behavior

To make it easier to understand these differences, we have developed a simple framework that uses these two characteristics to identify four different modes our digital habits can be in:

	UNCONSCIOUS	AWARE
UNDERMINES VALUES	*AUTOPILOT*	*SELF-AWARE*
SERVES VALUES	*AUTOMATIC*	*INTENTIONAL*

Each of your digital habits will currently exist in one of these modes and will shift into other modes over time. Generally, this shift happens in the following order:

Mode 1 is **Autopilot**. Your digital habits in this mode don't serve your values. You also lack any conscious awareness of them. This is a blind spot and therefore a real danger zone. Many digital habits start in this phase.

Mode 2 is **Self-Aware**. Your digital habits in this mode still don't serve your values, but you notice you keep doing them anyway. The key difference is that you have increasing levels of awareness of them (and unsurprisingly, this can feel pretty uncomfortable).

Mode 3 is **Intentional**. You are acutely aware that your digital habit was not serving you and this has driven you to change the behavior to align more closely with your values. This entails a high degree of conscious effort. This is not sustainable long term but is a powerful way to get the habit back on track.

Mode 4 is **Automatic**. Your digital habits in this mode are serving your values and you are able to rely on them with relatively little conscious effort. The good news about this mode is that you get maximum benefit with little cognitive cost. The bad news is that the habit is in danger of slipping back into Autopilot mode.

In a dream world, our digital habits would stay in Automatic mode, but the more we perform a habit, the more unconscious our behavior becomes and the more we are separated from the intention behind it—eventually shifting us back into Autopilot mode.

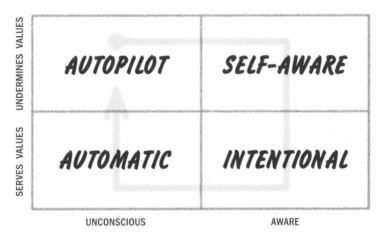

Typically, your habits will shift between modes in this cyclical pattern that returns to Autopilot.

Let's consider what this looks like in reality with an example of a classic trick that is often recommended early in your digital habits journey—removing your phone from the bedroom:

- In the **Autopilot** phase, you regularly scroll through social media before you go to bed and are not even consciously aware of it.
- In the **Self-Aware** phase, you are watching yourself scroll through social media and want to stop. Still, you just can't put the phone down, and you feel terrible about it.
- In the **Intentional** phase, you have become so aware of this disconnect between your desires and actions that you are spurred into putting your phone outside your bedroom. When you first try this, it is quite a disruption to your normal behavior and is highly intentional. Each

time you leave your phone outside the bedroom, it is notable, and this acts as a celebration and deepening of your intent to create a healthy boundary.

- In the **Automatic** phase, the phone being out of the bedroom has become a habit and you regularly benefit from it. However, with each repetition of the habit, you lose touch with the strong intent behind it.
- At one point, your phone inevitably sneaks back into the bedroom (it's just one night for your work trip, after all). The unconscious doomscrolling habits take hold again and you are back in the **Autopilot** phase. You could be there for months before things change again.

Bearing this in mind, the obvious question arises—how can you keep yourself in the beneficial part of the Automatic phase and stop yourself from slipping back into the Autopilot phase?

Keeping Digital Habits Intentional Through Practice

Sometimes, an Automatic behavior becomes too unconscious. There is a sweet spot where the habit is strong and you still have enough awareness of it that you can keep it in check. So how can you prolong this sweet spot? By moving back to an intentional mode, even briefly, with regularity.

Returning to our scenario of keeping your phone out of the bedroom: Once you enter Automatic mode, you leave your phone outside of the bedroom without any thought. If you can find a way to refresh how you do this, then the extra conscious effort required will help reconnect with your intention and keep it alive at the heart of your habit.

There are many ways you could do this: Changing the spot where you leave your phone every few weeks, adding a new note by your phone each week as you leave it outside identifying a reason that you value this habit, picking a new book you want to read and acknowledging that this habit is helping create the space to read it. Some of these ideas may sound good to you, and some may sound a little cheesy. The whole point is to experiment and find what works for you— use your creativity to find different ways of reconnecting with your intention and stick with the ones that make a difference.

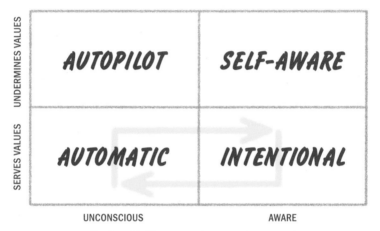

Your best digital life means moving between these two modes.

By doing this, you are strengthening your awareness of and intention for the habit regularly, but it's important to note this is not about completely undoing the habit—we still want to benefit from the automatic behavior to navigate the complexity of our digital lives. It's about doing just enough work to keep it alive and fresh.

Ultimately, this is a practice of watching your habits play out with awareness. In the same way that you need to keep exercising to stay fit, living your best digital life means revisiting your intention to keep your digital habits aligned with your values.

Summary

- A habit is an automation of our behavior. Your best digital life is one in which your digital habits align your behavior with your goals and values.

- The digital environment is challenging and slippery in five specific ways we have not evolved to deal with (yet), making it very difficult to cultivate digital habits that consistently work for us.

- Instead of thinking about digital habits as good or bad, it is more useful to consider whether they are intentional or not.

- Our habits exist in one of four phases: Autopilot, Self-Aware, Intentional and Automatic. It is easy for an Automatic habit to stop serving us without us even realizing it, which is why we need to keep checking in as a regular practice.

PART 2 Method

Understanding the principles from Part 1 is not enough—they need to be applied to your life. We've developed a four-step method that will help you put them into practice in a realistic and sustainable way.

The M.O.R.E. Method

Or, A New Way to Shift Your Digital Habits

For nearly 10 years, we have explored countless different ways of applying the principles of Part 1 to everyday life, working closely with digital habits "in the wild" to understand practically how we can all live our best digital lives.

Over this time, we have developed and honed a systematic approach that we have found to be particularly effective. A key requirement for this method is that it is not overly complex and therefore is memorable and simple enough to be applied consistently within the chaos of digital life.

This method focuses on consistently being intentional with your digital habits and finding creative ways to transform your relationship with tech into opportunities for personal growth, even in the most mundane and challenging depths of the digital trenches.

We have taught this method to thousands of professionals in some of the world's leading organizations, and they have put it to the test while working in incredibly demanding digital work environments. Time and again, it's proven to be an effective way of increasing their productivity, well-being and connection.

We've named it the M.O.R.E Method based on its four steps:

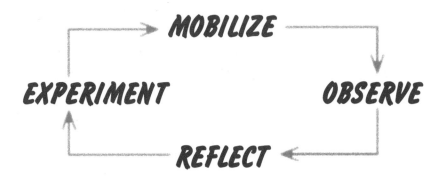

MOBILIZE

OBSERVE

REFLECT

EXPERIMENT

"Habit is the *what*....
A ritual is not just
the action but the way
we enact it—the *how*."

—Michael Norton

MOBILIZE.

Create moments of intention.
Embrace a growth mindset.

Living your best digital life relies on identifying unconscious digital habits that don't serve you and transforming them into intentional ones that do. But that's easier said than done—the problem with raising our awareness of our unconscious habits is that they're, well, unconscious! The trick is to find ways to regularly break out of autopilot mode and do something highly conscious with your mind. This is the point of the first step in the M.O.R.E method.

When you mobilize, you take a moment to raise awareness of your behavior and bring your mind into a space that is open to growth and change. By repeating this process—again and again—you increase your capacity to bring awareness to your digital habits themselves, allowing you to consider how you could transform them.

The mobilize step moves clearly away from unconscious habits by carefully using moments of ritual. A habit happens automatically, whereas a ritual is carried out with intention, mindfulness and meaning. Our lives are already filled with rituals: making a perfect coffee to start your day, celebrating your team's successes each month, placing flowers at the grave of a loved one on their birthday, ringing in the New Year with friends. The mobilize step uses this human convention of creating rituals to catalyze the process of building intentional habits.

Mobilizing rituals are often simple acts, such as rereading an inspiring quote, taking time to close all your browser tabs or deliberately placing your smartphone in a separate room before sitting down to eat. But they can transform an ordinary activity into a meaningful moment. And once you imbue an act with meaning and intention, you raise your awareness of it, allowing you to process it differently from those things you do passively or without a second thought.

A Practical Framework for Mobilizing

You could have two people doing the exact same thing, something as ordinary as clearing their desks to begin work. One person is solely concerned with the end goal—moving things so they have enough space to get their work done. The other is not just concerned with clearing space but also *how* they do it. Throwing old papers out methodically, one by one, each signifying mental closure on that project; placing a meaningful item that has nothing to do with work but which reminds them of what matters most; taking time to visually align each item on the desk so there's a feeling of order and unity. For the first, it's an automatic habit. For the other, it's an intentional ritual.

Each time you repeat a habit, it becomes more unconscious and distanced from the "why" behind the action. Each time you repeat a ritual, it creates a conscious reconnection to your "why" and brings it alive in your experience at an emotional level.

While some mobilizing rituals might seem complicated at first glance, they don't necessarily need to add extra complexity to your day—any of your existing, everyday actions can be transformed into Mobilizing rituals. You can draw on your posture and physicality, objects around you, sounds in the environment, spoken phrases or silent thoughts.

RITUAL ← **BEHAVIOR** → **HABIT**

INTENTIONAL   AUTOPILOT

> **LITTLE AND OFTEN** Small actions done with intention can be powerful. Your Mobilizing ritual doesn't need to be elaborate or take a long time. Think of a soccer player always touching the grass right before entering the pitch—it's a tiny moment, but one that connects them with their "why" as well as their belief in themselves.

MORE

1. Clarify Your Intention

When it comes to your digital habits, ask yourself:
- What matters to me?
- Why do I want to change?
- What benefit do I want to bring about?
- And for whom?

2. Identify a Moment

Look for moments in your day that mark a transition into a new situation. For example:
- The moment between waking and getting out of bed.
- The first time you sit down to start work.
- Setting up for a video call.

Choose one to use as the basis for your ritual.

3. Define Your Mobilizing Ritual

What actions naturally occur during your chosen moment? Select one or more of them to become your ritual. They could be:
- A single action, such as opening a laptop.
- A sequence of events, such as setting up a temporary workspace.

Link that set of actions with the emotional feeling related to your intention and wish for change. This is the blueprint for your ritual.

4. Practice Your Ritual

Each time your chosen moment occurs, this is your cue to intentionally engage in your ritual. As you go through the sequence of actions you identified, allow them to link your intention to your present situation.

Mobilizing Your Digital Habits

In psychologist Carol Dweck's book *Mindset: The New Psychology of Success*, she explores two different mindsets: fixed and growth. The main difference between them is simply belief: Those with a growth mindset genuinely believe they are capable of change. Dweck's research has shown that this belief itself plays a key role in an individual's ability to change and grow. Rituals are frameworks for consistently bringing us back into that growth mindset in which we believe in our innate ability to change. After all, our brains are plastic, meaning they keep changing until the day we die.

In reality, you have a mixture of beliefs and you move between these mindsets depending on the ups and downs of life, such as how well you slept last night or how out of control your digital habits feel. One large-scale study (with nearly 150,000 participants) found that globally, 30 percent of adults suffer from addiction to their smartphones. In light of studies like this, we can end up feeling quite hopeless.

From a growth mindset perspective, however, hopelessness is ultimately just another belief. Things may feel bleak right now, but if you keep trying to disrupt your habitual responses to the situation, your circumstances will change at some point.

Listening to inspiring podcasts and other motivating sources is particularly helpful for shifting your narrative and naturally strengthening your belief that change is possible. You must consciously make room to imagine what you're capable of. This is an art, and each time you mobilize, you increase your ability to work with your thought patterns and create a mindset conducive to change.

> **PRACTICE MOBILIZING** Near the beginning of each Practice in Part 3, you will find ideas for Mobilizing rituals to support your best digital life. Use them as a starting point to develop your own and keep trying different ones out until you find something that fits.

MORE

1. Clarify Your Intention

Jonathan recently wanted to create a new Mobilizing ritual based around his intention to create more mental space in his digital life. He took a moment to connect with what it feels like to not have your head filled with a million different things. He also tried to feel how strongly he wanted this for himself.

2. Identify a Moment

When looking for a moment to base the ritual in, Jonathan identified his morning shower. This was already a daily event, and those few minutes of freshening up his body felt like the perfect support for strengthening his intention for freshening up his mind too.

3. Define Your Mobilizing Ritual

Jonathan decided to connect the act of washing his hair with the intention of creating mental space in his life. He brought to mind his desire for change and made a mental connection between that and the act of rubbing the shampoo into his scalp. As the bubbles dripped down his forehead, he even began to imagine them as mental clutter falling away.

4. Practice Your Ritual

Now, whenever Jonathan takes a shower, he uses it as an opportunity to recall and refresh this intention for change. Sometimes it feels quite forced, but even then, it serves as a useful support to enter a growth mindset on a regular basis. He's even been known to jump in the shower again in the afternoon if he's particularly struggling to find mental clarity that day!

Three Core Skills for Mobilizing

1. Keep It Real

The way you mobilize needs to be personal and authentic to you. Sometimes this comes very naturally, especially if you are inspired or enjoying good life circumstances. At other times, especially if you are in a state of mind where everything seems hopeless or you feel nothing you do can bring about any change (we've all been there at one point or another!), then trying to forcefully override this feeling will not bring about the desired results. You need to be skillful with yourself, be kind and give space to your experience and beliefs while also finding playful ways to poke holes in it.

Through this you can learn to identify where your limiting beliefs may be holding you back. Dave Gray writes in his seminal book *Liminal Thinking*, "We construct our beliefs, mostly unconsciously, and thereafter they hold us captive. They can help us focus and make us more effective, but sadly, they also can limit us: they blind us to possibility." Identifying limiting beliefs and working to overcome them requires you to become open to the possibility that change is possible. You must consciously make room to imagine what you're capable of.

Throughout this book, we will be sharing real-life examples of Mobilizing rituals that could help you with this, but remember: These might not be the best fit for you. They are shared primarily to provide a model and starting-off ideas for designing your own rituals. A Mobilizing ritual must be meaningful to you, and it really doesn't matter what anyone else makes of it.

2. Course-Correct

The process of Mobilizing makes a core assumption that you know what matters to you. But this can be hard to uncover, and even once you have clarity on your intention (your "why"), it will keep changing. As humans, our situations change all the time—and as a result, the things that matter to us will change too. Unlike most GPS systems, however, we are not great at updating our route when things change. The habits that helped you in a previous situation will be hanging around, but may no longer serve you in your current one.

The beauty of a Mobilizing ritual is that it connects you to your "why" every time—it is a purpose-driven approach to behavior change. So when that "why," that purpose, has changed, you'll know that it's time to change your rituals too.

3. Aim High

When you mobilize, we encourage you to make your aspirations as big as possible. Don't hold back! Connect with the strongest sense of positive growth and self-fulfillment you can imagine and put this at the heart of your deepest desire for change. It doesn't even need to stop with you—you can also include the desire for others to experience a positive change as a result of your actions. By connecting with the intention to positively impact those around you (e.g., your family, your colleagues) through your practice of intentional digital habits, you will bring an even deeper sense of meaning and purpose to your journey of experimentation. This will help you stay on track, no matter how difficult the road ahead becomes.

"How we spend
our days is, of course,
how we spend our lives.
What we do with this
hour, and that one,
is what we are doing."

—Annie Dillard

OBSERVE.

Be open to new information.
Embrace a curiosity mindset.

Once you've taken the time to mobilize, you will be ready to make some changes! You might be tempted to jump straight into action, but that would actually be counterproductive. Before you dive in, it's incredibly valuable to spend time Observing your situation and behavior in order to see more clearly how your current habits are playing out.

As we explored in Principle 3, one key reason our digital habits are especially tricky to work with is that we lack conscious awareness of them. While we have a sense of our own habits, we often don't notice our actual behavior while it's happening because it's so frictionless and automated, and we are also unaware of when previously helpful habits have stopped serving us.

How do we improve our awareness? By becoming deeply curious. We can expand our awareness of our digital habits by investing time in exploring them by paying close attention. Only then can we hope to understand what is really going on.

Attention is the critical component, as where and how you place your awareness in any given moment can have a massive impact on how you perceive and interpret the world around you and your relationship to it. This is the very reason social media companies and dotcom advertisers continue to compete for your attention or even seek to manipulate it: They know how powerful it can be.

By becoming deeply curious about your experience, you start to retake control of your attention, building your capacity to choose where you want to place it. That's why the observe step is so crucial. Reclaiming your attention gives you clarity and focus, allowing you to create the conditions to make your digital habits work in your favor.

A Practical Framework for Observing

Perhaps the most challenging element of Observation is our capacity to concentrate. How can we see something clearly if we can't even keep our attention on it for more than a few seconds? We need to be able to keep our mind still enough that we can rest it wherever we are looking for as long as possible, which goes against the flow of our lives. This is a basic capacity of the mind that anyone can strengthen through the practice of mindfulness meditation.

You can do this by picking an object—it could be a part of your body, a houseplant or even something more subtle, like the sensation of your fingers on the glass screen of a device. Once you've chosen an object, the exercise is deceptively simple: Rest your attention lightly on that object, and whenever you notice that your attention has moved elsewhere, gently return it back to the object. That's it.

Of course, our minds are busy places and a session of placing your attention on an object rarely passes without a lot of internal distraction. Don't be put off by this though—this is exactly the point. When strength training, you need the repetition of lifting heavy weights in order to build your muscles. In the same way, each repetition of noticing you are distracted and returning your mind to your chosen object is the way you strengthen the muscle of concentration. It is the whole point of doing the practice in the first place.

> **LITTLE AND OFTEN** It's important to have a clear sense of when you begin and end your observation. We recommend short periods (1 to 5 minutes) daily. This is far more effective than a 30-minute session weekly. This is because we are building the muscle of attention, so regular repetition is the most helpful.

MORE

1. Check In

Get comfortable and find a position in which you are not slouching. Check in with your body, noticing any discomfort. Now check in with your mind, noticing any busyness, judgment or worries. Give them space. There is no need to change anything; you are simply acknowledging your current state before you begin Observing.

2. Choose Something to Observe

Choose your object—let's say it's your belly. Simply observe the belly rise and fall as you breathe. When the mind inevitably wanders away, invite it back to rest on your belly again. Whenever you notice you're attending to something other than your object, that's your cue to come back.

3. Get Curious

The heart of this process is curiosity, as if this were the first time you ever observed the object of your focus. Notice the various sensations, sounds and movements of your belly. Instead of using your predictive mind, stay open to surprise and allow reality to override your expectations. Stay alert to this process of discovery.

4. Keep Coming Back

There will always be lots of things trying to take your attention away when you are attempting to concentrate. When that happens, don't be too harsh on yourself or get caught up in commentary about how you became distracted (that's just another distraction in itself!). Simply bring the mind back to what you've decided to observe. Again and again. That's all you need to do—and as with any muscle, the more you do this, the easier it becomes.

Observing Your Digital Habits

The more you train the muscle of your attention, the easier it becomes to place it on any object you choose. Start with simple objects that aren't too unstable or distracting. Over time, you can begin to turn your lens of Observation on your digital habits themselves. There are countless ways you could observe your digital habits—but the key is to hold a deep sense of curiosity and draw on your experience of lightly placing your attention in one place.

When you observe your digital habits regularly, you will begin connecting the dots and noticing patterns. What kinds of situations make you crave your phone? Maybe you find that whenever people ask you a certain question, it creates discomfort and a desire to escape. These are valuable insights! Once you know, you can do something about it: You can craft a skillful response based on objective and nuanced facts rather than on a general impression of what is going on. The observe stage is all about getting the information we need to respond in a way that is most impactful for our specific situation.

Not All Curiosity Is the Same

When we're observing our own habits, Jud Brewer (a leading psychologist at Brown University researching habit change) speaks of two different types or "flavors" of curiosity coined by psychologists Jordan Litman and Paul Silvia: D-curiosity and I-curiosity. The D stands for deprivation, which is the impatient need-to-know state. The I stands for interest, the pleasurable aspects of finding out something new. D-curiosity is like a persistent itch that is uncomfortable with anything unresolved. It is looking for one convenient, simple solution that explains everything. On the other hand, I-curiosity is more like a flow state in which you are not hunting down a specific answer but falling in love with the process of observing with an open mind. This curiosity is comfortable in nuance and uncertainty and is energized by the fascination of letting things unfold in front of you, revealing their complex truth in unexpected ways. This is the type of curiosity to bring to your observation.

> **PRACTICE OBSERVING** In each Practice in Part 3, you will find suggestions for ways to strengthen your Observation skills and prompts to apply them to your digital habits daily.

MORE

1. Check In

Imagine you're sitting at a restaurant with your friends—people you deeply care about but maybe haven't seen in a while. As you're catching up, you feel this pang, an urge to reach into your pocket and check your phone.

2. Choose Something to Observe

This is your prompt to begin simply observing your desire to check your phone. Instead of getting distracted by reaching for it, or by excusing yourself to go to the bathroom and check it sneakily, try for a moment to simply pay attention to your desire to check the device.

3. Get Curious

Let yourself feel the impulse. Here, your own inner sensations become the object of observation. There is a part of you that is watching yourself. Notice how your feelings fluctuate from anxiety to anticipation to amusement or whatever else arises.

4. Keep Coming Back

You might notice thoughts such as "I think I'm really addicted!" or "I wonder what the basketball score is. Let me just quickly check it and then I'll get back to this 'Observe' thing!" The mind is swift to move from one topic to another. Gently bring yourself back into Observation mode, noticing all the ripples of thoughts and feelings.

Three Core Skills for Observing

1. A Beginner's Mind

Have you ever tried to draw something in front of you, say, a mug, and been disappointed that it doesn't quite look "right"? This misalignment of expectations and reality happens when we draw what we think is there as opposed to what we actively observe. By going back and looking more closely at the mug, you realize that the reality of the handle in front of you actually looks very odd! In this moment, you are seeing with fresh eyes—a beginner's mind—freed from the baggage of your mental concepts of what mugs "should" look like. As you update your drawing accordingly, the marks on the paper look strange, but the result feels much more realistic because you are now closer to seeing the mug as it is.

Observing with a beginner's mind is something we need to keep practicing again and again. In the same way that no one becomes Picasso overnight, you shouldn't expect to develop a master's eye in Observing your own digital life in a single afternoon. It's an active process. It requires patience. And practice. And a sense of humor.

Crucially, your observation must be fresh every single time. This is challenging because the same ultra-efficient mind that creates habits to conserve your mental energy will also attempt to take similar shortcuts in the looking process. The moment your observation becomes automated, you lose the ability to see what's in front of you as your conscious mind checks out. At this point, you are simply seeing your ideas about what is in front of you, not what is actually there. As the saying goes, "The map is not the territory."

2. Courage

Imagine you have a looming deadline but consistently find yourself procrastinating in various digital distractions (Wordle, anyone?) instead of actually getting down to it. It can be hard to get into Observation mode and watch yourself do that! You will need to tolerate the discomfort as you direct your curiosity to the heart of the raw and knotted feeling that is driving your procrastination in the first place. But it will be worth it. Observation allows you to take any experience ("good" or "bad") and benefit from all of it—nothing is off-limits. But this is easier said than done, because the act requires really looking at yourself, flaws and all.

MORE

Any habit—no matter how ingrained—can be changed, but only if we start with seeing it clearly. Some of our habits can be scary or unnerving or flat-out embarrassing. Observing can therefore be highly uncomfortable. It takes courage.

3. Non-Judgment

It is tempting to get drawn into making judgments when observing ourselves, especially when looking at what we believe to be unhealthy digital habits—but the goal is not to categorize your habits as good versus bad. The goal is to raise your own awareness of what you are doing, rather than comment on it or judge it. "I am reading my ex-girlfriend's Facebook posts," is an Observation. "That's a little desperate" or "I need to stop doing this!" is a judgment about your behavior.

To practice meaningful Observation is to practice keeping your inner critic at arm's length, giving yourself space to exist free of judgment as a human being simply being themselves. As you hone your ability to observe your behavior, you will find you're always learning something valuable, regardless of whether or not what you observe fits your preconceived ideas of "right," "comfortable" or "good."

Try acting like a researcher who has no agenda regarding what they observe—they are simply there to see reality more clearly and to record that data in a purely objective manner. Observation is about seeing clearly and arming ourselves with accurate information before making changes to how we do things. Remember: It's all useful information you can use constructively in the next step.

We do not learn from experience. We learn from reflecting on experience.

—idea attributed to John Dewey

REFLECT.

Ask questions and dig deeper.
Embrace an analytical mindset.

How often do you put aside time to reflect on your situation? Not the daydreaming type of reflection, but really placing something under the microscope of our attention. While you may often think about the people, events and priorities in your life, most of the time, you likely wander into that train of thought by accident—perhaps while doing the dishes, waiting for a bus or in the middle of the night when you can't fall asleep.

There is nothing wrong with any of these scenarios necessarily, but none of them allows for deep thinking. These ad hoc approaches leave the act of reflection to chance—it is still possible that you might start thinking deeply about your digital habits while waiting for a bus (especially if you have this book on your mind), but it's far more likely that you pull out your phone and do one of a million other things instead.

For this reason, the M.O.R.E. Method includes a formal reflect step, designed to help you gain insights into your digital habits in a reliable and structured way. Five minutes is all you need, making the step both simple and convenient. This will help you identify why certain habits arise, which of them are serving you and which are not.

If you followed the previous step (Observe) as outlined, you resisted the urge to judge or analyze whatever you were looking at. Now is your chance to do exactly that! But as with everything else in the M.O.R.E Method, we need to do it with intention. We are going to fully examine the things we've been Observing with our analytical eye, evaluating whether they align with our professional and personal values.

A Practical Framework for Reflecting

There's a phrase commonly attributed to Harvard biologist E.O. Wilson that sums up the crisis of the digital era in one sentence: "We are drowning in information, while starving for wisdom." But what did he mean?

Any question, regardless of its pertinence to our daily lives, can be answered with a simple "Hey Google." What is the capital of Australia? How many minutes are there in a week? How many solar panels would it take to power the world?

Having this much knowledge at our fingertips gives us the illusion of understanding everything, but in reality, we are merely parroting back the data points on our screens. In many cases, we aren't invested in the result so, just as quickly as it was summoned, the information is tossed aside to make room for the next data point. If you don't take time to reflect on what you've Observed in step 2, you run a similar risk of simply drowning in information about your own habits. Reflecting allows you to digest this information into your experience.

So how can you go about transforming the information that you've gathered about your digital habits in the observe step into something you can benefit from? You must go through a process of actively breaking that information down into a form that can be understood in the context of your personal goals and priorities and ultimately be experienced in your daily life.

INFORMATION ➤ UNDERSTANDING ➤ EXPERIENCE

When you understand something, you have your own unique interpretation of it and can articulate it in your own words. When you experience something, your interpretation is no longer just theory—it is validated by your current actions. Only then can you directly apply the understanding and benefit from it fully.

> **LITTLE AND OFTEN** Your week is 10,080 minutes long. Spending a handful of them reflecting can reap huge rewards for your digital habits. Try this formula and adjust based on your current capacity: Warm up: 2 minutes, Reflect: 5 minutes, Digest: 2 minutes.

MORE

1. Warm Up

Calm your mind by paying light attention to an object. You can use all the skills you've developed in the Observe step here or you can do some box breathing (see pg. 121).

2. Reflect

Focus on a question. This question should be different each time you reflect (see pg. 93 for an example), but its purpose is to examine something in more detail in a way that encourages your mind to think deeply about it without jumping to conclusions. Try asking more questions, turning the information over in your mind and looking at it from different perspectives. Whenever you notice you are thinking about something other than your question, simply return your attention to the process of reflection.

   In each Reflection session, you will either reach a point of insight and understanding, a point of confusion or simply feel mentally exhausted. None of these are the single correct destination, but they all signal a good place to end the session. Alternatively, you can set a timer.

3. Digest

Wherever you arrive (e.g., insight, confusion, exhaustion), rest in the atmosphere of that for a minute or two. Let the experience wash over you. If you've ever done yoga before, you could think of it like the period of Savasana (Corpse Pose) at the end of the session: After all the activity, you lay still for a few minutes and let all of the experience from the session settle and assimilate into your being.

Reflecting on Your Digital Habits

Information must be made personal because understanding is always, necessarily, subjective—it forms a direct relationship between you and the information. Let's take a single piece of knowledge as an example: "Multitasking is impossible." You've likely heard this fact before, but chances are that having access to this knowledge hasn't stopped you from writing an email to win that next big client while scrolling through a Grubhub menu and participating in a group text. For a statement like "Multitasking is impossible" to have a tangible impact on your behavior, you must first understand exactly what it means. We do this by asking questions, such as:

- What does it really mean that you can't pay attention to two things at the same time?
- What is actually happening in your mind, moment by moment, as you do two things at once?
- Are these things true in your own experience?
- How could it benefit you to do one thing at a time?

Once you've asked questions like this, you've made the knowledge personal to you. From there, you can draw insights and relate them to your own situation and needs. After examining it more fully, you might begin to feel the negative impacts of something like multitasking in a more personal way than when you simply "knew" trying to do it would be fruitless.

As you repeat this process, this understanding will then begin to bleed into your experience. To continue the example, the next time you find yourself trying to do two digital tasks simultaneously, you might recall your reflections, which would cause you to experience your insights in real time. Only then are you able to benefit from the original information—it has become truly assimilated into your being, and you can begin to implement behaviors like task-batching with confidence and ease.

> **PRACTICE REFLECTING** Toward the end of each Practice in Part 3, you will find prompts for Reflecting on your digital habits in various areas of your life. Make some time to try them out and bring in reflections of your own to go even deeper.

MORE

1. Warm Up

Watch an object (or practice some box breathing) to settle your mind and focus it, ready for reflection.

2. Reflect

What is happening in your mind, moment by moment, as you do two things at once? When reflecting on this, at first your mind may feel blank, like a deer in headlights. Be patient with yourself and keep returning to the question. Slow down, make no assumptions and consider it in relation to your own direct experience.

You could make it experiential by attempting to actively do two things with your mind at the same time (such as spell a word and do some simple math) and try to see more deeply what is actually happening. Is it possible to do them both at the same time or not? Do you do one then the other, or do you jump between them?

Only by taking the time to relate this back to your own experience and forming your own opinions about it can you turn the information you're focusing on into an understanding that will benefit you more deeply.

Through this process, you may have an insight, like a penny dropping. If so, then this is a good point to move on to the digest phase. Alternatively, if you feel like you don't have the mental energy to continue, then you're ready to move to the next phase of this process.

3. Digest

Wherever you end up, notice the atmosphere in your mind, whether it be confusion or exhaustion, and rest your attention lightly in that. Let the experience seep into your being for a few moments before carrying on with your day.

Three Core Skills for Reflecting

1. Reflect at the Right Speed

When reflecting, you may quickly come to a conclusion, but chances are that the thinking that got you there is flawed. In 2002, Daniel Kahneman won the Nobel Prize in Economic Sciences for his finding that humans have two fundamentally different modes of thinking:

- System 1, which is automatic, impulsive, reactive and fast.
- System 2, which is conscious, deliberate, considerate and slow.

Both of these systems are essential and we use them together throughout the day. However, we spend up to 98 percent (!) of our time using System 1 to make quick decisions using mental shortcuts called heuristics. The danger of overly relying on heuristics is that we can often quickly jump to the wrong conclusions.

Slowing down your thinking to avoid these biases is a real challenge and they can easily fly under our radar. This makes it difficult to understand just how these biases shape your experience. But one way we can make them explicit is by reflecting on optical illusions like this one:

The middle strip is, in reality, a single solid color (cover up the background and see for yourself!). Even once you know this, your System 1 thinking is so strong that you continue to see the middle strip as being lighter on the left and darker on the right. Bearing this in mind, when reflecting to break information down into understanding and experience, engage with the work of analyzing what you've observed so that you are not jumping to any wrong conclusions. This is best done in short, regular bursts.

2. Use the Five Whys Technique

Asking a "why" question to reflect on your digital habits can be revealing (e.g., "Why do I check my email so often?"). Answering why isn't always complicated ("Because!"), but getting beyond a standard, snap response and analyzing until you get to the truth is more challenging.

The Five Whys is a technique that was developed in the 1930s by Sakichi Toyoda (founder of Toyota) as he sought to identify underlying causes of problems that arose on the manufacturing floor. This technique—which simply involves asking "Why?" five times in a row—can be a really useful tool for your reflection sessions. When you find an answer (e.g., "Because I can't do my job if I don't check my email all the time"), you can then go deeper by asking "Why?" again: "Why can't I do my job if I don't check my email all the time?"

Continue until you can't go any further (aim for at least five whys to ensure you're not stopping too soon). This can be a powerful process that reveals some of our assumptions or blind spots and can help move our reflection forward in a deeper way.

3. Be Persistent

You won't always reach a significant new insight each time you do this. Play the long game. There will be some sessions of reflection where you can't keep your mind focused at all. In others, you will be able to stay focused on the question, but you won't be able to articulate any answers—it will feel impenetrable and unsatisfying (much like the feeling of not being able to find the end of the roll of Scotch tape).

This is not only OK, it's to be expected. It can take time to break information down into smaller pieces, so if early attempts feel fruitless, trust that you are making progress (it's just not visible yet). Keep returning to the reflection with some regularity, and at some point, you will gain a new insight—and this moment of understanding can have huge potential to shift your habits.

"There is no such thing as a failed experiment, because learning what doesn't work is a necessary step to learning what does."

—Jonas Salk

EXPERIMENT.

Challenge your beliefs.
Embrace a disruptive mindset.

By now, you will have more clarity and insight into your own digital habits through the work you've done in the Observe and Reflect steps. You will have increased your awareness of your unconscious habits and may be at a point where you are ready for change. The Experiment step helps you make this change by disrupting your existing unconscious digital habits and making a small but highly intentional change to your behavior.

The key here is that the changes are small. You are not looking to redesign your entire relationship with tech overnight but to make a very specific intervention based on your insights into your own digital habits. Making focused and intentional incremental changes will isolate any potential benefits you experience, giving you confidence in that approach as a tool you can rely on in the future.

The experiments you run will sometimes be things that are completely new to you, but just as likely, they will involve techniques or hacks that you've heard of elsewhere but never got around to actually trying. For example, an experiment could be deciding to try using your phone's Do Not Disturb function to limit notifications during work hours. You could try augmenting something that works for you in one area of your life ("No phones at the dinner table") in a different one ("No phones in the living room, to prevent the habit of second-screening"). Alternatively, you could come up with a novel approach that seems like it might work for you ("No tech of any sort on Tech-Free Tuesdays").

The experiment phase is all about exploring new approaches to see what helps and what doesn't while acknowledging (like any good scientist) that even experiments that don't prove your hypothesis still have value. By repeating this process over time, you will be able to keep shaping your digital habits in ways that best serve you.

A Practical Framework for Experimenting

The experiments that you run will be very personal responses to real experiences you've had with your digital habits. One of the first that Menka ran was to change the home screen on her phone by moving all of her apps into one giant folder. This wasn't an easy decision (Menka is the kind of person who takes great joy in seeing a neatly organized home screen), but she often found herself engaging with one of these apps without realizing she'd even picked up her phone. To slow down the sequence of events, she wanted to make it less convenient to find the right app. She'd open up the folder and type the name of the app, giving herself a moment to catch up with what her hands were doing. F-A-C-E...wait, did she really want to open that app? Over time, this approach has evolved to keeping the apps she wants to use more often directly accessible on her home screen, throwing all the others into the all-in-one folder in which she has to actively look for them.

Jonathan has returned many times to running an experiment that involves not engaging with any technology for the first hour of his day, using this time to do things like go for a walk, read a book or enjoy a slow breakfast. Each time he runs the experiment, he rediscovers the immense value that a slow, disconnected start brings to the rest of his tech-heavy day. Inevitably, over time, new digital habits creep in that interrupt this routine. So he revisits the experiment every three to four months and disrupts his behavior again each time.

> **LITTLE AND OFTEN** While it can be tempting to run lots of different experiments at the same time, we recommend choosing one and doing it for a short period of time. Sticking with one experiment will make it easier to evaluate the results. You can then initiate another M.O.R.E. loop and keep running small experiments over the long term.

MORE

1. Form a Hypothesis

Each experiment will ideally start with a simple hypothesis. The theory you are testing could come directly from something that you've observed or reflected upon. Or, it could be something you intuitively want to try. It can be helpful to formulate your theory in an if-then statement: "If I do X, then I believe Y will be true."

2. Plan Ahead

Consider what you'll need to get started. Will you need any equipment that you don't have right now? Do you need to prepare something in your environment? Perhaps you need to give your spouse or co-workers a heads-up. Don't leave any of these things to chance—build in time to get it all set up before you begin.

3. Choose the Duration

Decide when the experiment will begin and end and find a way to ensure you stick to it. You may want to add it to your calendar or set an alarm for the beginning and end. If you don't do this, it will be difficult to see the results clearly as the experiment slowly fizzles out (or doesn't even get started in the first place!).

4. Evaluate the Results

Once the experiment is done, look again at your original hypothesis and see what the results are telling you. Maybe your hunch was right. Or maybe you were wrong, and you've discovered something new and surprising about yourself. Evaluate the results with an open-minded, curious attitude to maximize your insight. Often, this will lead you to form a new hypothesis, which can inspire you to come up with a new experiment. Don't just be another person with an opinion—test it out for yourself.

Experimenting With Your Digital Habits

When choosing an experiment, you may find yourself coming up with lots of different reasons that you can't give that particular one a try. For example, the experiment outlined on the opposite page is all about checking your email at certain times of day. Perhaps that sounds appealing, but your job requires that you respond to clients promptly. That is, of course, a very valid reason why it could be difficult for you to attempt such an experiment.

However, there is always a way to hack or redefine an experiment in a small way that makes it possible to run. For example, if you need to constantly reply to emails the moment they arrive, perhaps you could experiment with finding a single hour in your week where you can close your inbox (you might ask a colleague to cover for you or try the experiment on Friday afternoons if they're pretty quiet, anyway).

Alternatively, you may decide that attempting the experiment is impossible during the workweek but that it could be worth trying in your personal time. If you are sending immediate replies to emails all week at work, that habit might be spilling over into your personal emails in a way that is unhelpful.

Whatever the case, the trick is to find a version of each experiment that is realistically manageable for your own situation and yet takes you far enough outside of your comfort zone that it offers the potential for a positive change.

PRACTICE EXPERIMENTING At the end of each Practice in Part 3, you will find suggestions for Experiments to disrupt your digital habits in various areas of your life. Try them out, hack them to your own needs or invent new ones!

MORE

1. Form a Hypothesis

"If I schedule three one-hour sessions a day to check my email and make sure my inbox is closed at other times, I believe I will be able to finish my urgent project without dropping the ball on communication."

2. Plan Ahead

Before starting, add "meetings" to your calendar specifically for getting email done so that this time can't be double-booked. Treat it like a real meeting and turn up on time. Let your colleagues know you will be running this experiment and therefore may not be as readily available as they have come to expect.

3. Choose the Duration

You could decide to run the experiment every day for a week and revisit the number of email sessions you will have each day based on your experience of the day before. This allows you to stick to a clear plan for the day but also make micro-adjustments based on what you learn throughout the week.

4. Evaluate the Results

On evaluation, you might find that it was difficult to stick to the sessions every day, but on the days you did, you were undeniably more focused on deep work. You could decide to run the experiment again the following week, but this time, try more regular email sessions of 30 minutes each to see if that's a better fit for you.

For even more detailed ideas on how to run each experiment, check out the Digital Habit Lab (see pg. 233 for more info).

Three Core Skills for Experimenting

1. Visualize Ahead

Disrupting your behavior is hard work, and many obstacles can come up when trying something new. One study showed that when people are trying to adopt a new exercise routine, even with a motivational session to support them, only 38 percent went on to try it. The same study found that by simply visualizing yourself doing the exercise ahead of time, the success rate rose to a massive 91 percent.

To help make sure you actually try out your experiments, you can visualize yourself doing them by using the following formula: **At [time], in [place], I will [action]**. For example, "At the start of my shift, when I sit at my desk, I will add a sticky note to my phone to help reduce unnecessary distraction." It may seem that such a simple thing couldn't possibly make a difference, but we've been consistently amazed by the impact.

2. Run Experiments Multiple Times

Don't be afraid of running the same experiment multiple times. This is a good idea for several reasons. You may have noticed on pg. 71 that the M.O.R.E. Method is a loop. Finishing an experiment sets you up to begin the process all over again. Each time you complete a M.O.R.E loop, you deepen your awareness and understanding of a habit. This will likely include uncovering new information as your experience allows you to become aware of some finer subtleties within your behavior. You may also change your approach slightly based on your experience the first time around.

Additionally, as we've mentioned, your context is always changing. You may have experimented in the past with keeping your phone out of your bedroom and reaped the benefits. But over time, as life circumstances change, perhaps it has snuck back in and taken up residence on your nightstand again. Returning to an experiment over and over will help you keep your digital habits on track, no matter what life throws at you.

Even if an experiment shows that a certain strategy is effective, it can take the mind a while to get on board. The geocentric model of sun and planets all rotating around the earth was embedded into many ancient civilizations, and despite multiple different scientists proving otherwise, the new model of everything rotating around the sun took many centuries to be accepted. Prevailing views can be stubborn. Give yourself time to see things differently.

3. Suspend Your Disbelief

There are likely many hacks and methods you've heard about that could help you with your digital habits but that you've never gotten around to doing. It could be that you don't have time, don't believe they would really benefit you or aren't ready to commit to a whole new method or routine.

This is why we use the term "experiment"—you are simply trying something out for a limited period of time with no expectations of a particular result. There is no commitment to do this new thing forever. Think of it as trying it on for size for a limited time in order to understand more deeply how it may be of benefit to you.

The best thing about this is that you don't need to believe that an experiment will actually be effective in order to try it! Usually, people decide beforehand whether something will work out or not, and this can be very limiting. When it comes to disrupting our behavior, it's our blind spots that most need to change.

"Practice isn't the thing you do once you're good. It's the thing you do that makes you good."

—Malcolm Gladwell

Bringing It All Together

Now that we've introduced the four steps to the M.O.R.E Method, it's time for you to put it into action. That said, there are a few pointers we've learned through experience that we think would be helpful to share first.

M.O.R.E. Is a Practice

The M.O.R.E Method brings the most benefit when we do it regularly—much in the same way that we must continue to exercise if we want to stay fit. No matter how good your digital habits may seem today, it's only a matter of time before this will change. A backslide might occur due to a shift in outer circumstances, such as more responsibility in your role, the required adoption of a new company communication tool or the release of a new piece of technology that changes how or where (or when) you work. Or it could be related to a change of internal circumstances, such as feeling tired, anxious or upset.

Whatever the case, these adjustments in your context can occur at any time, and they will all impact your digital habits in unpredictable ways. The M.O.R.E. Method has been designed to be resilient to all of these inevitable changes and to always offer you a simple and obvious next step to help bring clarity and agency to your digital life. For this reason, we strongly believe developing a regular M.O.R.E. practice is one of the greatest skills you can teach yourself for the future. The primary benefit of focusing on the practice rather than specific habits is that it allows you to let go of the pressure of needing to always have "perfect" digital habits because you understand that this is not the point.

The value doesn't come from trying to hold down a rigid (and unsustainable) concept of a perfect digital life but rather to use the natural ebb and flow of your behavior as a raw material to increase your self-awareness and agency. This is what will really help you navigate any obstacle the digital world puts in your way.

The other benefit is that the practice will always be relevant, whether that's when VR headsets (or smart contact lenses) become as ubiquitous as smartphones, when AI easily matches full human intelligence or in the distant future when new technologies we can't even imagine yet are disrupting our lives.

Each of the M.O.R.E. steps appears simple at first glance, but actually doing them is tough! Don't let that put you off, though—a practice, by definition, needs to be applied. If these steps remain a nice idea that you are inspired by but ultimately never try, then they cannot really benefit you. The practice requires some work on your part (unfortunately, you can't hire someone to do this for you!). It doesn't need to take long, but ideally, it should be something you do with consistency.

M.O.R.E. Is Not Strictly Linear

While the M.O.R.E. Method can be understood as a step-by-step process that forms a repeatable loop, it can also be applied in a way that's more organic (or, if you prefer, intuitive). Try to resist the urge to get caught up in worrying too much about whether you are doing things in the right order. It may be that once you've finished Reflecting, you decide to jump back and continue to observe some more before experimenting. That is absolutely fine, although it is easier said than done if you're a textbook overthinker. Cut yourself some slack. Every new habit feels odd at first.

You can also have multiple M.O.R.E. loops running at different levels. You could be working on several different areas of your life testing out several different experiments. Some might be quick ones that are done in a day, others could take much longer, say, a monthlong experiment in keeping your phone out of the bedroom.

The other non-linear aspect of the M.O.R.E. method is that every time you run an experiment, you disrupt your behavior and change your situation. Thus, when you next mobilize, you will be in a different place. You have deeper insight into your digital habits and more confidence about what methods do and don't work for you. Every time you complete the loop, you are growing and moving into new territory. Even when things may not appear to be changing outwardly, you are evolving internally. It's more like a spiral!

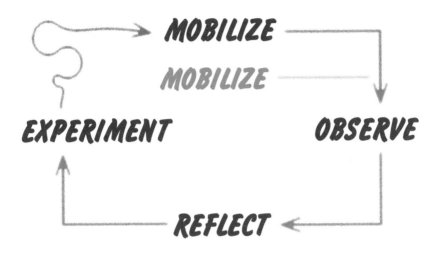

M.O.R.E. Can Be Multiplayer

When it comes to digital habits, it's easy to fall into the trap of thinking it's a solo project. But much of our behavior plays out in relation to others. Consider your digital habits around email and instant messaging. Then consider the same digital habits of your colleagues. Both of you can work on your own individual digital habits, but there is also the messy area in between: the cultural digital habits of your team and organization.*

For this reason, once you have started to work on your own digital habits, you may find it's necessary to try to bring those around you on a similar journey. In truth, this is a topic for another book, but there are a few pointers we can share that will be especially useful for anyone in a leadership position.

Everyone is different, and there are no single digital habits that work best for everyone. It takes time to discover what works best for you as an individual, and the same is true for a team. In order for you to be able to do it at the team level, you must first empower those around you to have the skills to develop their own M.O.R.E. practices. Until this happens, establishing a M.O.R.E. practice at the team level will be nearly impossible.

*For more on digital habits for organizations, see pg 233.

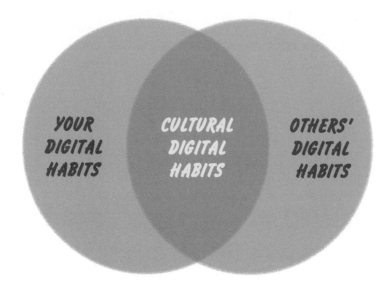

YOUR DIGITAL HABITS   CULTURAL DIGITAL HABITS   OTHERS' DIGITAL HABITS

The main task is to create space for others to begin to reflect on their own digital habits and create a shared cultural language around digital habit behavior change. Telling others to do this doesn't work—they need to discover it for themselves. Consider the following tips:

- **Start With Yourself** Establish your own M.O.R.E practice and stick with it for a good while before looking to others.
- **Show Your Work** Find ways to share your own M.O.R.E journey with others to create a natural sense of curiosity in them.
- **Speak From Your Own Experience** Always fall back on your own experience and learning, showing an understanding that what works for you may not work for them.
- **Be Vulnerable** Don't be afraid to share the things you struggle with. Many people are surprised to learn that others experience similar difficulties and struggles, and this is a powerful way to get them invested.

It is worth mentioning that this approach works well with families, too, especially when even the youngest member of the household is empowered to hold others accountable. As we all know, those close to us can often see our unhelpful habits more clearly than we can.

The Goldilocks Approach to M.O.R.E.

It's often the case that any kind of routine or practice that benefits us tends to fall away just when we need it most. Exercising regularly and eating well are foundational to our well-being, but when life gets busy and we are stretched, it's ironic that we often feel we can't make proper room for them. In the same way, your M.O.R.E. practice will be of immense benefit when your digital life is feeling very squeezed, but counterproductively, this is the time you are most likely to stop doing it! To help with this, you can take a Goldilocks approach and make time to define what small, medium and large versions of how you practice M.O.R.E. look like. Your small version will be the least elaborate—the bare minimum required to keep it going when the pressure is on. Your medium and large versions will be more elaborate and you can apply them when you have more time on your hands.

When life is completely chaotic, stick to your small version and prioritize Mobilizing for a short duration and do it as often as you can. Observing can be more casual, and Reflection can be one five-minute session a week. Fall back on an experiment that you know has helped you consistently in the past. Keep everything as manageable as possible to help you ride out the storm, but don't drop it altogether. Those five minutes of reflection could be just what you need to help take back control of your situation.

When your routine is closer to normal, apply your medium version by sticking to a consistent, manageable routine as much as you reasonably can. That could look like one minute of Mobilizing each morning, five minutes of Observing each day and 15 minutes of Reflecting at some point in the week, all as a means of running a single experiment.

When things are particularly stable and spacious, apply your large version of the practice and use this opportunity to spend more time reading books and going deeper into exploring supporting topics that will inspire you in the long term. This comfortable lull is also a great time to try out some of the more esoteric experiments out there.

Consider what your small, medium and large versions of M.O.R.E. would look like for you, then write it down so that when time is scarce, you don't drop the M.O.R.E. practice altogether.

PART 3 Practice

Your best digital life doesn't happen by mistake—you need to practice it. The following six practices will help you build intentional digital habits across areas of your life that contribute significantly to your overall well-being.

PRACTICE 1

Having a Body

Or, How to Live in Your Own Skin

The 1909 short story "The Machine Stops" by E.M. Forster details a dystopian world in which humanity has been forced to retreat from the surface, with individuals across the earth living in isolation belowground. Travel is permitted but is unpopular and rarely necessary. This is because a mechanical network—the Machine—connects every single person and allows them to communicate and share ideas. As a result, this has essentially become their only activity. The humans in Forster's tale have placed so much value on the direct consumption of information and ideas that their bodies have become something of an inconvenience. This devaluation of the physical causes human bodies to become enfeebled—described as small, pale "swaddled lump[s] of flesh." Even sex is detached and mechanized, a vile necessity. This loss of physicality is so detrimental that the protagonist's son (who seems to be the only person questioning the state of affairs) decides to reclaim this lost sense by doing something quite unorthodox: walking up and down the railway platform outside his room. Through this physical activity, he rediscovers the true meaning of words like "near" and "far"—relative terms defined by the limitations of human physicality: "Man is the measure. That was my first lesson. Man's feet are the measure for distance, his hands are the measure for ownership, his body is the measure for all that is lovable and desirable and strong."

When this was written just over a hundred years ago, it was pure science fiction. Today, it feels as though Forster were somehow peering directly over our hunched shoulders and into our present—where technology has empowered us with information but also weakened our sense of physical self.

Remember That You Have a Body

Considering how central our bodies are to our everyday experience, it's remarkable how easy it is to forget we have one. Take a moment right now to identify anyone in your immediate environment who's using a screen (yourself included). Where are they at this moment in time? Of course, it's true that they are physically present, but at the same time, they are almost entirely in their heads. Their minds are fully engaged in whatever is stimulating them on the screen. Apart from a deftly swiping or rapidly clicking finger, their body is largely still. Look closely and you'll find clues that support this: observe their posture, reduced movement (if any) and the general lack of awareness of their body and surrounding environment.

As we described in Principle 1, digital technologies extend the mind's capacity. But we also explained that the mind is more than just our thoughts—it includes our whole subjective experience of living in a body. Like the characters in Forster's story, technology expands our capacity for conceptual thought and does little else. It does this to the detriment of our connection with our physical self. It takes our minds to places that are unrelated to where we are physically—a vast expanse of spreadsheets calculating

MORE

MOBILIZE

*"Few of us have lost our minds,
but most of us have long ago lost our bodies."*
—Ken Wilber

1. Clarify Your Intention
Take a moment to consider how your relationship with tech impacts your sense of embodiment and physical well-being. Then, try to identify an area of this relationship you'd like to improve—this could be something quite specific or a broader aspiration for yourself, such as, "I'm the kind of person who finds ways to stay more connected to my body in my digital life."

2. Identify a Moment
Here are some examples to get you started.
- Getting out of bed in the morning
- Opening your email
- Eating lunch
- Brushing your teeth at night

3. Define Your Ritual
For example, whenever you open your email, take a deep breath in through your nose and release it slowly through your mouth. Do this three times while aspiring to always breathe this fully in your digital life.

4. Practice Your Ritual
Throughout the day, keep an eye out for your cue to practice your ritual and use this moment to link your intention to your present situation.

SEE PG. 73 FOR MORE ON HOW TO MOBILIZE

future dreams, the time-warped destination of a nostalgia-fueled trip down memory lane, a netherspace where ninjas slice fruit—which can leave us feeling distanced from ourselves.

When discussing such subjective experiences, it's useful to refer to firsthand accounts of what this actually feels like. For example, consider this post from a since-deleted Reddit account on the r/digitalminimalism subreddit:

> Its [sic] hard to explain, but you know when you wake up in the morning and the rain is quietly pattering on the roof, and you just feel so cozy and alive in that moment... that kind of feeling never happens to me anymore. As soon as I wake, my mind is flooded with a bunch of thoughts. I feel like my mind is very overactive. As a kid and teenager, I would often feel those magical moments like waking up with the rain on the roof, waking up early and sipping your coffee and wondering about the day and about life, etc. Just little things where you feel really present and alive.... I've felt this way for a few years now, and as a kid this was never an issue. I also used to be much more creative, and just "feel" things more. I really don't know what to make of this. I definitely feel that technology is to blame partly, but I want to know what others think. I wonder if the constant flood of information from the internet is making my brain become more overactive and taking me out of my body?

You Experience the World Through Your Body

For many of us in the West, our worldview has been shaped by the influence of philosophers such as René Descartes, who instilled the conventional wisdom that understanding the world is a purely intellectual pursuit. The famous phrase "I think, therefore I am" leapfrogged the physical form, painting a picture in which we stand detached, observing and analyzing the world inside our minds without ever dirtying our hands with the messiness that is our physical state of being.

Over the years, there have been an increasing number of critics and skeptics of this viewpoint, and in the mid-1900s, a few key philosophers put forward the idea of phenomenology—a philosophy of experience that places the ultimate source of all meaning and value in the embodied experience of human beings. This group of thinkers analyzed the various ways that our bodies shape our thoughts and how we experience our conscious activities. This in turn has inspired a field of study called embodied cognition—a wide-ranging research area drawing from and inspiring work in psychology, neuroscience, ethology, philosophy, linguistics, robotics and artificial intelligence. Each of these disciplines is unified by the idea that the body (or the body's interactions with the environment) shapes our thoughts.

Experientially, interacting with the world through our entire being (as opposed to being caught up in a flood of thoughts) is what helps us reconnect with moments such as the cozy sound of rain falling on the roof. But there are very practical implications, too. Writing by hand has been shown to increase your ability to recall information at a later date. Next time you want to remember something—maybe it's the name of a new colleague or the name of that Italian restaurant you went to last week—try writing it down rather than typing it into a device.

Bring Your Mind Back to Your Body Again and Again

So where does your mind go when you get lost in your head? Just about anywhere other than where you actually are. This is what psychologists refer to as a wandering mind—one that is thinking about what *isn't* going on around you, instead contemplating events that happened in the past, might happen in the future or may never happen at all.

As we will discover in Practice 2, which explores attention, it is quite natural—necessary, even—for our minds to wander (it helps us identify threats, make plans and function in the world). But that doesn't mean that the more we mind-wander the better. In fact, a 2010 Harvard study has revealed that excessive mind-wandering typically makes us unhappy.

In the study, Harvard psychologists developed an iPhone app that contacted 2,250 volunteers at random intervals to ask how happy they were, what they were currently doing and whether they were thinking about their current activity or about something else that was pleasant, neutral or unpleasant. It turns out that, on average, about 47 percent of most participants' waking hours were spent thinking about what wasn't going on. In other words, we spend nearly half our day disconnected from our embodied experience—our real present life. *Half* our day!

The researchers found that people were happiest when making love, exercising or engaging in conversation—all activities that require us to be fully present in our bodies (or at least not scrolling our TikTok feeds). Participants were least happy when resting, working or using a home computer. That's not to say using a computer will always make you unhappy, only that it is conducive to mind-wandering. The more you engage with digital devices, the higher the chances you'll be pulled out of your embodied experience. And the less time you spend in your embodied experience, at least according to the research, the unhappier you'll be.

So what can we do about this? While there will be some benefit to distancing yourself from technology for periods of time, this is not a practical solution for the majority of our day. Instead, try experimenting with bringing your mind back to your body again and again throughout the day.

What does it mean to come back to your body? Simply doing things that help ground you in the experience of your physical self. Your body is a collection of different senses and systems (e.g., digestion, respiration) and is capable of all sorts of activities. By consciously engaging all three—senses, systems, activities—in brief, regular intervals between tech use, you

OBSERVE

1. Check In

Take a few deep breaths. Notice the sensation of your breath as you inhale and exhale. Allow your breath to become slow and natural.

2. Choose Something to Observe

Imagine your attention is like a laser, slowly scanning the length of your body. Starting at the tip of your head, lightly place your attention on different parts of your body as you scan downward.

3. Get Curious

At each stage, notice what information is there.

- Do you notice comfort or discomfort?
- What sensations arise—hot, cold, tingling, numb, relaxed, tense, aching, sore, energetic, lethargic?
- What's happening inside? Do you feel any movements? Hear any noises?

Move slowly and be thorough in your Observation.

- Observe the top, middle and bottom (e.g., the tip of your ear, the inside of your navel, your littlest toe)
- Observe the front and back (e.g., front of thighs, back of thighs)
- Observe the space between things (e.g., the space between your nose and your mouth, the gaps between your fingers)

Once you've made it to your toes, bring your attention to your whole body and rest with that sensation for a while.

4. Keep Coming Back

When you get caught up in mental commentary during the practice, simply return your attention to your body.

SEE PG. 81 FOR MORE ON HOW TO OBSERVE

can go a long way to increasing your sense of physical presence throughout the day. By applying the M.O.R.E. Method, it is possible over time to become more aware of the moments when technology is keeping you caught up in your mind and disconnected from your body. In turn, this will help you apply the methods and experiments we explore in this chapter to keep grounding yourself in your fully embodied experience.

How Your Inbox Steals Your Breath

Breathing is arguably the very first independent and autonomous act of our lives, but unlike our other involuntary bodily functions (e.g., digestion, heartbeat), it is unique in that we can choose to override the natural pattern of our breath at any time. This skill is surprisingly useful, allowing us to speak at a higher or lower volume, sing or play musical instruments. Incredibly, doing so can even influence our state of mind. Researchers have found that our breathing patterns interact with our vagus nerve, which carries signals between our brain, heart and digestive system. It controls many of the involuntary changes in our bodies, such as how much saliva we produce, how we speak, what food tastes like and our mood. Our bodies switch into "rest and digest" mode or "fight-or-flight" mode depending, to a large degree, on how we're breathing.

Intentionally engaging in slow, deep breathing has been shown to reduce anxiety and stress. Similarly, shallow breathing and breath-holding trigger a stress response. It may be tempting to think you have already mastered breathing (after all, you've kept yourself alive this long without any conscious effort), but the truth is not all breaths are equal, and we pick up many bad habits over the years. There's a pretty good chance you engage in unhealthy, shallow breathing regularly. You might be doing it right now.

In 2007, author and ex-Microsoft executive Linda Stone began to notice that her breath became very quiet and shallow whenever she was reading and responding to emails. She had been suffering from a chronic respiratory infection, which was the only reason she was examining her breathing at all—most of us would never really notice it. This led Stone to conduct a study, monitoring people's heart rates and breathing while they checked their email, the results of which revealed she was not alone. Roughly 80 percent of the people she observed were periodically holding their breath or slowing it down in some other way. Stone described this finding initially as "email apnea" and expanded it later to "screen apnea" because this disruption in breathing happens nearly anytime we're engaging with a task that requires a screen.

In some ways, this should not be surprising. Our inboxes are, after all, often a great source of stress and anxiety, which (it turns out) is one of the major drivers of shallow breathing. Our vagus nerve kicks off a chain of physiological changes to divert resources to help us focus. The more unexpected the stimulus—for example, getting a Slack message from your boss out of the blue—the more likely the body is to perceive it as a threat. This creates a vicious cycle where stress causes shallow breathing, which in turn engages our fight-or-flight system and deepens our state of stress.

Next time you're at your screen for a period of time, observe if you are holding your breath or breathing through your mouth (an indicator of shallow breathing). Reflect on what you find. Do you fall into the 80 percent of shallow breathers or the 20 percent who don't suffer screen apnea?

Come Back to Your Breath With Box Breathing

One simple but powerful method you can use to counter screen apnea is an aerobic exercise called box breathing. Box breathing has its roots in the pranayama yoga tradition dating back to roughly 800 B.C., but it has gained popularity in the modern era through its use in military and medical settings. The United States Navy SEALs began using box breathing to improve mental focus and calm in high-pressure situations as well as to prevent panic attacks.

The practice involves inhaling for a certain count, holding the breath for the same count, exhaling for the same count and holding the breath again for the same count. This creates a "box" pattern of four equal sides, hence the name "box breathing." Try it:

1. Inhale slowly through your nose, counting 1, 2, 3, 4.
2. Hold your breath for another count of four.
3. Exhale slowly through your nose for a count of four.
4. Hold your breath for a count of four (then repeat this whole cycle anywhere from two to 20 minutes).

If you're new to box breathing, ease into it with just a few minutes a day and gradually increase the duration as you become more comfortable. Box breathing can be used as a tool to help you manage stress and anxiety at any time. This will remind your body that you are fine and send positive messages through your vagus nerve to help you relax. Over time, as you become more aware of your breathing, you are less likely to have long spells of shallow breathing.

To experience the full benefits of box breathing, it's important to practice it regularly. Use the M.O.R.E. Method to identify moments when it could be most beneficial (such as when tackling your inbox, between back-to-back virtual calls or replacing a couple of minutes of social media scrolling), then run an experiment, setting aside a few minutes each day to practice box breathing to make it a part of your daily routine.

Come Back to the Wisdom of Your Body

In the spring of 2024, Menka was engaged in a charity fundraiser with a goal of walking 100 miles. One day, while speed walking with her sister-in-law who'd brought her baby along in a stroller,

MORE
REFLECT

1. Warm Up
Spend a couple of minutes using the observe technique to watch an object (or practice box breathing) to settle and focus your mind to ready for reflection.

2. Reflect
Now swap out the object you were focusing on (e.g., your breath, an object, a sound) for a question, for example:
When do I feel MOST/LEAST embodied?
- What does being embodied feel like?
- When did I last experience that feeling strongly?
- Why was I able to feel so embodied in that instance?
- What does being disembodied feel like?
- How does my sense of embodiment impact my digital habits?

3. Digest
Wherever your reflection ends up, notice the atmosphere left in your mind: Is it one of clarity, confusion or exhaustion? Whatever the case, simply pay attention to that feeling and let this experience seep into your being for a few moments before carrying on with your day.

4. Make it Your Own
Try reflecting on things that particularly inspire or intrigue you. Here are a few suggestions to get you started.
- What assumptions about my body does my technology use create?
- Who knows me better—me or my smartwatch?

SEE PG. 89 FOR MORE ON HOW TO REFLECT

Menka offered to help push (to achieve a slightly greater workout). An hour later, when she looked at her smartwatch, it said she had only done 2,000 steps. She looked at that figure, slightly puzzled for a moment, before concluding that, evidently, they weren't walking as fast as she had thought. But when her sister-in-law declared she had completed 8,000 steps, Menka figured out what was going on! The smartwatch doesn't count steps if your wrists are not moving (in this case, because she was holding the stroller handles). This wasn't Menka's first time using the smartwatch or her first time speed walking, and yet she had doubted her sense of reality based on the information presented to her by a piece of tech. She had deferred to its authority, even on a subject in which she could rightly claim some expertise.

Why do we ignore our bodies and defer to the perceived wisdom of an app or piece of tech? In part, it's because we've come to trust the latter far more than the former. In a world driven by big data and large language models, we're subconsciously digesting vast amounts of information while slowly losing confidence in the information our bodies can provide—the sort of information that has served our species for millennia. It's become natural to defer to data rather than instinct, but ironically, there's data that suggests your instincts are good!

In their book *mBraining*, Marvin Oka and Grant Soosalu bring together several insights from neuroscience over the last 30 years that describe the systems of our body as not just having one brain but many. If you consider what a brain is made of, you will find groups of cells that create infrastructure (e.g., neurons) and collections of chemicals called neurotransmitters (e.g., dopamine, serotonin). Collectively, they act as a network that processes all kinds of information, manages memory and coordinates your nervous system and related movements. These neural nets are not just found in our heads, it turns out, but also around our hearts as well as in our stomachs (that's right: Gut feelings actually come from your gut). Here's how Soosalu and Oka define these systems and how they interact with one another:

- **The Gut Brain (Enteric Brain)**
  While still in the womb, your gut brain develops first, then your heart brain and, finally, your head brain. Your gut contains more than 500 million neurons, similar to the number of neurons found in an octopus's brain, and can operate independently of any input from the head brain. The gut brain also uses each of the same 100+ chemicals found in your head brain.

- **The Heart Brain (Cardiac Brain)**
  Your heart brain contains roughly 40,000 neurons and shares many hormones with your head brain, used for bonding and social interaction. As Oka and Soosalu write in *mBraining*, in specific situations, the heart brain can "function independently of the head brain and it can learn, remember, feel and sense." The heart brain works in tandem with the head brain and has a direct impact on shaping our behavior.

- **The Head Brain (Cephalic Brain)**
  This neural network is made up of more than 86 billion neurons. It receives information from the heart and gut brains alongside all other sensory inputs and coordinates our nervous system while performing executive functions such as reasoning, deciphering meaning and language expression.

A Note on the Quantified Self

If you are familiar with concerns about how technology impacts the body, there's a good chance you will also be familiar with the tech solutions to it. As we discussed in Principle 2, the tech industry seeks to offer a solution for every problem we face. Not walking enough? Here's a fitness watch that will remind you to get up and move when you've been at your desk too long. Worried about your posture while you're using your smartphone? Here's a smart vest that will beep and vibrate around your shoulders when you slouch.

This tech-driven approach to biofeedback—using wearables and nanosensors to generate data about the body and share it with us so that we can try to alter our habits—has been used to track many aspects of our embodiment, from heart rate to depth of sleep to cholesterol and blood sugar levels. These helpful, sometimes life-transforming developments are all part of what has become known as the Quantified Self movement. Using such tech can boost our awareness of what is happening with our bodies, opening up a whole new world of information we might otherwise miss or never know, even while paying close attention. These apps and wearables have been a boon in many respects, but because they inevitably feed us data, ratios, metrics, charts and screenshots, they put us squarely in our head brains. We are using third-party (which is to say external) information to understand our body's functions rather than focusing on getting firsthand, real-time intel directly from the source.

In some ways, as we become more reliant on these devices, we become not only less aware but less capable of tuning into our bodies. We may wait for phone notifications to tell us to move rather than letting our stiff muscles tell us it's time for a stretch break. The tools designed to strengthen a mindful connection to our bodies can paradoxically distance us from our direct experience and knowledge of them—or, at the very least, give us a false intimacy with that connection. That is not to say we shouldn't use them to understand our bodies better—these are excellent tools. But quantifying the self is not the same as experiencing what it means to be alive and is not what we mean when we talk about the practice of getting out of our heads and into our bodies more. Take time to Experiment and find the right balance for you.

MORE

EXPERIMENT

Notice Your Posture

Bring regular awareness to your body throughout the day, especially while working, in order to increase your physical and mental well-being.

Avoid Blue Light at Night

Use built-in tools on your devices to protect your sleep cycle and avoid unknowingly exposing yourself to blue light at the wrong time.

Eat Meals Without Screens

When eating, have a conversation with someone, spend time with yourself or take your lunch outside. Savor every bite.

Keep a Tech-free Bedroom

Make your bedroom a no screen/device zone so the clear function of the space is to obtain high-quality sleep.

Take an Inbox-Free Vacation

Create the conditions to ensure that you can fully switch off from checking email while you are taking a vacation or day off.

Charge Your Phone Away From Your Bed

Move your phone charger out of arm's reach to the opposite side of your bedroom. For bonus points, relocate it to another room altogether.

Practice Box Breathing

Engage with this controlled breath work technique regularly to rewire your nervous system via slow, deep diaphragmatic breathing patterns.

Navigate Without GPS

Take a different route or visit somewhere new without relying on an app to guide you. Plan your trip, use your senses and ask for directions!

Leave Your Device Behind

Strategically choose a few moments in your day to create significant distance between yourself and your connected devices.

Avoid Early Morning Tech Use

Protect and prolong the natural space and autonomy you have upon waking by delaying the first moment you engage with your devices.

SEE PG. 97 FOR MORE ON HOW TO EXPERIMENT

Slouching Makes You Feel Negative

A good indication that tech has caused us to recede into our thoughts is our physical posture. As we lose awareness of our body, our posture becomes increasingly hunched, slouched and slumped—as if our minds have taken flight and all that is left is a pile of bones and muscle. While this can be hard to spot in ourselves, it's hard to miss when observing others. Whether it's people on the train or waiting at the airport, it can be quite sobering (and sometimes disconcerting) to look around you and witness the hordes of bodies mindlessly contorted around their screens.

Beyond being an indicator of not being embodied, poor posture can also be harmful to our mental and physical well-being. It's probably not news that the ergonomics of how we set up our keyboard, mouse and monitors has a direct impact on our physical health. But you may be surprised to learn that research has also shown that your posture has a direct bearing on your mental state. In a San Francisco State University study, a group of students was shown two distinct postures: slouched and looking down versus sitting upright with shoulders pulled down and back. They were then asked to assume one of these two postures while recalling a good experience as well as a bad experience. The students then promptly switched postures and tried to recall the same good and bad experiences. The results are revealing: 86 percent of the students in the slouched position were able to more easily remember their negative experiences, while 87 percent of the students in the upright position found it easier to remember positive experiences.

The study concluded that therapists should teach clients posture awareness and to sit more upright in the office and at home as a strategy to increase positivity and decrease depression. Interestingly, posture is also another major contributor to shallow breathing, as a hunched back makes it difficult to draw deep breaths from our diaphragm, which results in us using only the top portions of our lungs.

Come Back to Your Posture With Awareness

If you wish to explore the impact of your digital habits on your physicality, try using reminders to regularly note your posture. If you sit down to write emails for an hour, try consciously adopting a good posture at the beginning, then set an alarm to check in on your posture when finished. Repeatedly checking in with your posture like this, even for a moment, can raise your overall awareness of your physicality over time. Each moment you notice you are slouching is an opportunity to gently adjust yourself.

Adjusting your posture to change how you feel is an outside-in approach backed by substantial evidence. And there are many more. Cognitive behavioral therapy, for example, has a practice borrowed from contemplative traditions called the half-smile, in which you bring a subtle, tiny smile to your face and hold it for about 10 minutes. This simple act can improve your mood. Some people find it helpful to also smile with their eyes. Normally, a smile is a result of joy, but what this and similar practices show is that it can work the other way around, too. Choosing to smile, rather than doing so reactively, can do wonders for your mood.

Many of these beneficial behaviors have unconsciously become part and parcel of how we interact with others. For example, most of us smile while talking to another person face to face (actively or subconsciously), which means there's a passive benefit to the active decision to converse with someone in person. The rapid adoption of technology often misses a few of these subtle tricks that evolution has taken so long to embed into culture. Next time you draft an email, try it out—bring a gentle smile to your eyes and lips, and we bet you'll feel a little more embodied (and relaxed) as you type.

Screens Give You Jet Lag

Our eyes have a special type of photoreceptor cells (melanopsin-containing retinal ganglion cells, aka mRGCs) that are highly sensitive to light. Unlike the rods and cones responsible for vision, mRGCs don't help us form images—they simply track the light entering our eyes. They are the most sensitive to short-wavelength light, which humans see as blue light. Upon sensing blue light, mRGCs send signals to the part of the brain in the hypothalamus that's considered the body's master clock and that regulates the body's circadian rhythm. This, in turn, leads to higher levels of cortisol (the stress hormone), which makes us more alert and awake. Conversely, when there is little to no blue light, this causes higher levels of the sleep-inducing hormone melatonin, which helps us relax and prepare for bed. This circadian pacemaker also changes other variables, such as our core body temperature, memory and a whole host of other body functions, so that we wake and sleep in a cycle that matches day and night. And it's not just our eyes doing this work—the tissues in our face and the skin elsewhere on the body also have different kinds of light-sensitive proteins tracking whether it's day or night.

This whole system is so well-honed and sensitive that exposure to even a few minutes of bright light in the evenings can throw us off. Our digital screens are increasingly brighter than natural daylight in order to be visible in direct sun. This brightness is really helpful when navigating on a bright day—less so when watching a video in bed at night. Exposing yourself to blue light at the wrong moment is equivalent to giving yourself 1.5 hours of jet lag. In response to public concern about this, most digital screens now have apps or native options that automatically dim the blue end of the spectrum toward the end of the day, leaving the screen looking more red—like an evening fire—which is not as stimulating and confusing for our bodies.

That said, just because we have options to avoid exposing ourselves to blue light at the wrong moment doesn't mean we remember to use them regularly. It may be that you are not aware of them or perhaps you found them intrusive when trying to watch a movie that one time, so you turned them off and fell out of the habit. We highly recommend running an Experiment across your various devices to try limiting your exposure to blue light and learn for yourself in which moments it can benefit you most.

Your Body Is *MORE* Than an Inconvenience

Sit up straight. Drink more water. Get enough sleep. With so much caretaking required, it can seem like the body is simply an inconvenience. Many Silicon Valley tech bros seem to feel this way and are replacing the inconvenience of making meals by ingesting Huel (a nutritionally complete milkshake) instead. But approaching the body in this way makes for a slippery slope.

Philosopher David J. Chalmers wrote a book called *Reality+* predicting that in the future, most people will live inside virtual reality and that the pursuit of the physical may come to seem a novelty or even a fetish. In this scenario, bodies will simply be an administrative burden. Echoing the scenario Forster envisioned more than a century ago, Chalmers writes in *The Guardian* that "people will need real food, drink and exercise, and perhaps even the odd glimpse of daylight, to keep their bodies from withering away." He is partly taking the stance that this is inevitable, so we may as well face the music. But we certainly don't believe it is desirable and hope it is not inevitable (this is where optimism comes in!) to live as though we don't have bodies.

What is the best way to come to your own conclusion on this? Use the M.O.R.E. Method to run a few Experiments in which you live your digital life with awareness and appreciation of the body and compare it to the times you've ignored your body.

PRACTICE 2

Paying Attention

Or, How to Do One Thing at Once

As the sun began to set on NASA's lab in California one afternoon in the summer of 1997, a group of engineers huddled in excitement around their monitors. They were looking at images of that same sun rising over the landscape of an entirely different planet. These were the initial images being beamed back from the *Mars Pathfinder* rover, the robotic spacecraft sent on a historic probe mission that gave us the first panoramic images of the surface of Mars. "This is way beyond our expectations," said Brian Muirhead, flight systems manager at the lab. "The whole day has just been extraordinary."

The next day, however, things were not looking so sunny. The rover had begun to display some erratic behavior, stalling over even the simplest of tasks. Start-stop-start-stop. The engineers quickly entered emergency mode, hoping to identify what was going wrong. As they pored over the debug logs, they were relieved to see that all the rover's systems were operational. And yet, the rover was just sitting there, as if it were trying to decide what to do next!

As it turns out, this wasn't far from the truth. In order to function autonomously over the vast distance between Earth and Mars, the rover was programmed to run through a list of tasks, each of which were given a priority level. It would complete them in order based on the relative urgency of each task. The team discovered that every time the rover would begin to make progress on a task, it would update its list and determine that another task was a higher priority. In doing so, since it was built to only work on one task at a time, it would abort the previous task and start on the new one. This pattern kept repeating itself, holding the rover in an endless loop of distraction, repeatedly switching between tasks and never completing any of them.

Computer scientists call this "thrashing." Maybe you call it "a typical Monday." Labels aside, one thing is certain: In a digital environment where everything is made to feel like a priority, it's not always easy to know where we should be placing our attention.

How We Set Goals and Why Attention Fails Them

For most of the 3.7 billion years that life has existed, sentient beings haven't set goals. We have reacted reflexively to whatever was occurring in the moment thanks to a system called the perception-action cycle: We see something and we respond. This behavior is referred to as "bottom-up" because it is driven solely by sensory information, without the need for conscious thought. Our ancestors heard a rustle in the bushes and immediately ran to hide from a potential predator. Today, you look at your to-do list and immediately run to Instagram to distract yourself from the rising sense of anxiety.

More recently (and by that we mean in the last 35,000 to 100,000 years), human brains have developed more sophisticated neural processes known as executive functions. These higher-level cognitive skills allow us to regulate our emotions, organize information, make decisions and formulate plans. In

MOBILIZE

"Tell me what you pay attention to
and I will tell you who you are."

—José Ortega y Gasset

1. Clarify Your Intention

Take a moment to consider how your relationship with tech impacts your ability to pay attention. Then imagine how you would like this to change—this could be something quite specific, or a broader aspiration for yourself, such as, "I'm the kind of person who chooses what I pay attention to in my digital life."

2. Identify a Moment

Some examples to get you started:
- Picking up your phone for the first time that day
- Opening your web browser
- Seeing someone else distracted by their phone
- Observing a moment of beauty around you

3. Define Your Ritual

As an example, whenever you spot a moment of beauty around you, pause to recognize that it's only possible because of your attention. Then make a mental resolution to protect your attention and only invest it in the things you want to see more of.

4. Practice Your Ritual

Throughout the day, keep an eye out for your cue to practice your ritual and use this moment to link your intention to your present situation.

SEE PG. 73 FOR MORE ON HOW TO MOBILIZE

other words, they allow us to stop being purely reactive and set our own goals.

These goals—behavioral scientists call them "top-down" goals—allow us to act with intention. They pause the perception-action cycle, creating the required space for deliberate action. When your to-do list gives you anxiety, instead of defaulting to the fight-or-flight response of procrastinating on social media, your executive functions help you choose a different path: "Take a deep breath and let's tackle these tasks one at a time."

Your executive function is a bit like a great manager. It doesn't actually carry out the goals but rather defines them and outsources them to another system in your brain: your cognitive control. This is a collection of three interrelated systems that actually roll up their sleeves to do the work: attention, working memory and goal management. They work together to help accomplish the task at the top of your to-do list. For example, let's say you're writing an urgent report:

- Your *attention* allows you to focus solely on what is relevant to the report.
- Your *working memory* holds context in your mind to write consistently and coherently.
- Your *goal management* system exerts the required self-control to stay on track.

In short, your cognitive control accomplishes your goals by paying attention to a specific task and keeping it in mind while deprioritizing other goals. It's a marvel of evolution that this system exists but, due to the human limitations of our cognitive control, it also doesn't always work as intended. This is because our ancient bottom-up system is still active, working alongside our sophisticated top-down behavior, and it directs attention toward particularly important events (such as potential threats or rewards). This push and pull is in play regardless of what you are doing!

In these moments, your attention experiences an internal tug-of-war between your intentional top-down goals ("Ignore your inbox and focus on this important project") and your reactive bottom-up reflexes ("Actually, I need to deal with this anxiety-inducing email before things get worse")—with the end result being an increase in stress (and often a to-do list that's longer than the one you started with).

The Two Types of Goal Interference

There is an official term for this affliction: goal interference. This is when you reach a decision to accomplish a specific goal (e.g., check the time) but something else diverts you from doing it.

Consider the following series of events Menka recorded when attempting to find out what time it was:

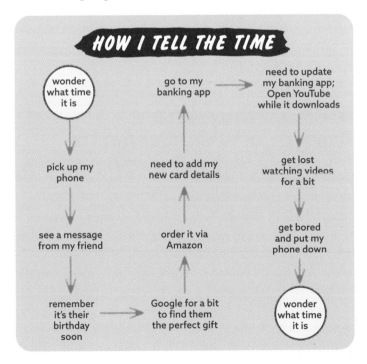

Notice how often goal interference derailed her from the intended task. Does this scenario feel familiar? The convenience of the smartphone offers countless pieces of information (entirely unrelated to telling the time) that can capture our attention. These can initiate completely new goals (like buying a gift), which we will inevitably also get sidetracked from completing. Our attention is helplessly directed from one thing to the next, and we only realize it when we come up for air.

In the thick of it, all goal interference feels the same, but in actual fact, it comes in two different forms: *distraction* and *multitasking*. Together, they're the reason you constantly feel like you aren't able to focus on and accomplish the items on your to-do list—even the ones you really care about.

By applying the M.O.R.E. Method, it's possible over time to become more aware of the mechanisms of this interference as it's happening. In turn, this will help you find methods that can protect and strengthen your attention, allowing you to feel more in control and be more effective. To start, it's important to gain more clarity on the differences between distraction and multitasking.

Defining a Distraction Depends on What Your Goal Is

Picture yourself diligently crafting a presentation for an important pitch. At that moment, there is a huge amount of information around you that has nothing to do with the task at hand. Internally, it might be the intrusive thought, "I wonder if I have any new comments on my Tweet." Externally, it could be the dissonant chime of a Microsoft Teams notification. What's important to point out here is that neither the thought nor the notification are considered distractions by themselves—it depends entirely on the context. If your job is in social media management, then checking Twitter is likely to be highly relevant to your current task. Or, if your goal is to collaborate with remote

MORE

OBSERVE

1. Check In

Begin by taking a few deep breaths. Notice the sensation of your breath as you inhale and exhale. Allow your breath to become slow and natural.

2. Choose Something to Observe

Here is an observation practice to try out when you are working—paying attention to your current task. Before you start observing, clearly define what your task is. Then, as you perform your task, continue to pay attention to the task and notice whenever any distractions arise. They could be outer sounds or events or inner thoughts, feelings or emotions.

3. Get Curious

Be curious about the inevitable distractions that arise. Mentally acknowledge each one as you become aware of it: thinking about your next meal, a notification, an itch on your leg, a colleague stopping by for a chat, the strong desire to drop what you are doing and go sit outside in the sun, quickly checking your email.

4. Keep Coming Back

Each time you notice a distraction, it's an opportunity to return to your task and strengthen your muscle of focus. This can become a micro-moment of celebration—celebrating that you noticed the distraction, celebrating the rich variety of distractions that can arise, celebrating the deeper insight into your digital habits, celebrating the opportunity to use the moment of distraction to build your muscle of focus. At the same time, there is no need to make a big deal of this celebration—simply return to your task and await the next distraction!

SEE PG. 81 FOR MORE ON HOW TO OBSERVE

colleagues in real-time, then the Teams notification could be crucial. Instead of distracting you, these chimes help keep you on track!

As Nir Eyal points out in his book *Indistractable*, "You can't call something a distraction unless you know what it's distracting you from." This insight can hit hard because it emphasizes that we are often busy at work without actually having a clear sense of what our current goal is. What feels like drowning in distractions is actually just a lack of clarity about what you are currently meant to be doing. Once you realize this and take a moment to define your current goal, dealing with distractions becomes significantly easier.

That's not to say defining your current goal will prevent distractions—quite the opposite! In our digital lives, we process the equivalent of a staggering 34 gigabytes of data each day in our leisure time alone. Of this information that's coming at us all day long, 99 percent has nothing to do with the goal we're currently engaged in. That may sound hopeless, but thankfully, we have two ways of dealing with it. One of them is an aspect of our cognitive control called attentional filters (more on this shortly), and the other is to create conditions that make it easier to identify distractions as they arise, before they get a hold of us and pull us off track.

Deflect Distractions With the Pomodoro Technique

We wrote this book using the Pomodoro Technique. Judging from our experience running digital habits workshops, roughly a third of you reading this book have heard of it before—but only a few of you practice it regularly. It was created by Italian software development CEO Francesco Cirillo, who used a kitchen timer (shaped like a tomato, or "pomodoro" in Italian) to break up work sessions and protect his attention from distractions.

While there are useful books and courses that teach the technique at length, the principles are incredibly simple and can be learned in seconds:

1. Define what goal you will work on next.
2. Set a timer for 25 minutes and work only on your chosen goal.
3. When the timer ends, take a break for 5 minutes, then repeat from Step 1 with another 25-minute timer.
4. Take a longer break of about 30 minutes after every four Pomodoro intervals.

When practicing paying attention in your digital life, we highly recommend you try the Pomodoro Technique with different types of tasks and situations and observe what works best for your situation. You may find this varies from week to week.

Remember: The technique only works if you regularly define your current goal, making it much easier to notice when a distraction occurs. If you are working away for several hours without using the Pomodoro Technique, your attention can slowly be diverted from your original goal without you noticing. But when you explicitly re-state your goal every 25 minutes, it helps add real clarity to what you are doing.

The breaks are as important as the focused sessions. Knowing you have a break coming up soon can help you jump-start those more difficult or tedious tasks. It makes it easier to resist the urge to follow a distraction when it arises—you can always tell yourself that you'll be able to attend to the distraction on the next break.

Make sure to use your break to do something that will help rejuvenate your attention. If you are trying to remember that you have a body (see Practice 1) you might want to move, stretch, breathe or look as far into the distance as possible through the nearest window!

Distractions Can Be Useful

When designing your digital life, it can be easy to slip into a mindset of trying to eliminate every single distraction, but this is not the point: What matters is how you deal with and manage distractions that arise. Distractions are inevitable—you can't control everything that happens in your environment! Plus, we actively need them to survive—if distractions were completely ignorable, you would potentially be missing life-threatening situations as they arise. Without being cognizant of what else is going on, there could be a fire in the room next door as you remain in deep focus mode, with your noise-canceling headphones on, adding the finishing touches to a presentation! Likewise, there are hundreds of distractions definitely worth ignoring.

The more you practice noticing and labeling distractions when they arise, the easier it will become to not get caught up in them. After you've labeled it, the distraction will stop provoking anxiety. It can even act as a way to strengthen your focus on your current task. When you hear a notification and can instantly discern that it's irrelevant to your current task, in that moment, you are being clear about what your current task actually is. The distraction has therefore become a *reminder*, keeping you on track.

Still, some distractions will inevitably break through, and you'll fall victim to the second type of goal interference: multitasking.

Demystifying Multitasking

Multitasking is when—instead of getting diverted into a completely different task—you make the conscious decision to simultaneously engage in more than one task at the same time. This happens when a distraction is compelling enough that you decide to engage with it alongside whatever else you are currently doing.

REFLECT

1. Warm Up

Spend a couple of minutes using the observe technique to watch an object (or practice box breathing) to settle your mind and focus it, ready for reflection.

2. Reflect

Now swap out the object you were focusing on in the warm-up (e.g., your breath, an object, a sound) and, in its place, focus on a question, for example:

Why do I feel so distracted in my digital life?
- Is it the specific technology I use?
- Is it the way I use the technology?
- Is it a lack of clarity about what I'm doing?
- Is it because I'm not setting boundaries?
- Is it because of my internal thoughts and emotions?

3. Digest

Wherever your reflection ends up, notice the atmosphere left in your mind: Is it one of clarity, confusion or exhaustion? Whatever the case, simply pay attention to that feeling and let this experience seep into your being for a few moments before carrying on with your day.

4. Make It Your Own

Try reflecting on things that particularly inspire or intrigue you. Here are a few more suggestions to get you started:
- Is multitasking actually possible?
- What are the times when I feel most/least distracted?
- What do I want to pay attention to?

SEE PG. 89 FOR MORE ON HOW TO REFLECT

Picture yourself preparing a presentation. Multitasking can manifest in various forms:

- **Internally** You hit a stumbling block in crafting a sentence, and this friction leaves you vulnerable to a distracting thought that pops into your head about the dinner you are having with friends later. Multitasking occurs when you actively choose to follow that thought and creating your presentation starts to regularly alternate with thoughts about the dinner: what you will wear, who you will see and what to order.

- **Externally** To try to take the edge off the intensity of the work, you decide to turn on Netflix and play *Friends* episodes in the background. Now, you're multitasking between writing the presentation and being entertained. *"Oh, nice! This is the one where Joey puts on all of Chandler's clothes. Could he be wearing any more clothes? No, he couldn't. Hilarious. Where were we? Oh, yes—the dinner. I mean, the presentation."*

Research has shown that multitasking is actually impossible. The term is borrowed from computer science because computers are built to do things in parallel. But, as we saw in Principle 1, our brains are not computers. It is impossible for us to parallel process information if both goals require cognitive control. While we may have the ambition to do two things at once, the reality is that we end up switching rapidly between each task, which has a cognitive cost.

The aftermath of rapid task switching is noteworthy—accuracy dwindles for both tasks and completion time escalates compared to a sequential approach. Studies underscore a fascinating paradox: Avid multitaskers often overestimate their dual-task proficiency, a serious rift between perception and reality. The habitual nature of multitasking exacerbates this disconnect, creating a widening gap between perceived effectiveness and the tangible output of tasks. We all think we're really good at it because we perform rapid task switching all the time. But the truth is, any time we split our attention, we lose seconds. Minutes. Often hours. Hours we could have spent completing the thing we set out to do in the first place. And that time adds up.

Task Batch Your Distractions

Have you heard of task batching? It is a way of supporting your attention by intentionally grouping similar tasks and doing them one after the other instead of spreading them throughout the day. You can task batch many different actions, such as replying to emails, filing expenses and so on. As you work through a group of batched tasks, you reduce the chances of thinking about or working on any task that's not in that group. This helps you work more efficiently because your brain takes time and energy to switch between different tasks.

Why not try task batching with the activities you know tend to distract you or tempt you into a multitasking fallacy? One experiment we encourage you to run is to use task batching to deal with the spontaneous urge that regularly arises to search online for a piece of information. This is often a common cause of multitasking because it's so easy to do. You know what we mean—it could be checking tomorrow's weather or finding the birthday of your favorite celebrity or researching the potential salary you could earn with your next promotion. Thanks to the convenience of search engines, we can query any of these things at any time. But chances are that now is not the optimal moment.

Instead, you could try jotting these search engine queries down in a notebook and returning to them later in the day after you have completed your main tasks. As usual, this can be incredibly challenging since the habitual desire to resolve an unanswered question can be very strong. But each time you write down a search engine query for later, you free up a degree of mental energy and also strengthen your attention, which will help you stay focused on the task at hand.

If you are anything like us, when you do finally get around to doing those searches later on, you may realize you don't actually care about many of them anymore, saving you distraction, effort and mental stamina all at the same time.

Pay Attention to the Right Things

Given the amount of information and stimuli flying around, you may be curious to understand how you can focus your attention on anything at all! The answer is through a tremendously valuable collection of neurons that are commonly referred to by neuroscientists as attentional filters. We are not capable of consciously attending to everything in our experience, as it would be overwhelming to our limited cognitive functions. As a result, the brain filters out anything it deems irrelevant to the task at hand, helping us choose where to aim our focus.

A bit like *Mars Pathfinder*, attentional filters assign hierarchical values to different stimuli based on how relevant they are to the task at hand, directing your attention to the most important ones. If you are hungry, you will be more aware of food in your vicinity than other objects (your awareness of smells is heightened, for example). If you are reading a book on public transportation, you will be blissfully unaware of the hustle and bustle around you. When looking at a *Where's Waldo* book, your attention will try to block out anything that is not red and white with glasses.

Attentional filters are a real superpower, allowing us to cope with the richness of the present experience in a practical and effective way. However, digital technologies can confuse our filters by flooding our experience with many things that are perceived as high priority in any given

EXPERIMENT

Use the Pomodoro Technique
Set a clear goal, then break your work into chunks with a beginning, middle and end.

Restore Your Attention
Experiment with a simple mindfulness technique for short daily sessions to create space and build your muscle of attention.

Delay the Urge to Search
Note your search engine queries as they arise, then set aside specific times of the day to look these up at once.

Put a Sticky Note on Your Phone Screen
Place a reminder with a short message on your screen to help you notice when you pick it up and ensure you are using it intentionally.

Schedule Email Sessions
Block out periods of time in your daily schedule exclusively for dealing with your inbox, then don't engage with email outside of them.

Use an Egg Timer
No need to rely on a phone for basic timekeeping while cooking— use a kitchen timer so you can maintain your focus.

Wake Up to an Alarm Clock
Set an alarm clock to wake you up in the morning (instead of your phone) so you aren't immediately tempted by your screen.

Turn on Airplane Mode
Support your attention by using focus modes on your device that block incoming call or notifications.

Embrace the "Dumb" Phone
Try a phone that deliberately lacks certain functions to help you stay focused on what matters.

Activate Grayscale Mode
Without color, everything is less emotive and appealing. You can do this permanently or during certain times of day.

SEE PG. 97 FOR MORE ON HOW TO EXPERIMENT

moment. Think of a screen full of red notification badges that are all equally urgent at first glance—this manipulation of what appears to be most important can create situations that disrupt our attentional filters and make it harder to stay in control of our focus.

Your Smartphone Has Hijacked Your Attentional Filters

The best example of technology messing with your attention in this way is your smartphone itself. While your attentional filters judge the relevance of most stimuli based on your context, some special information—like the sound of your name or the word "fire"—carries a privileged status in all contexts. It is associated so strongly with our sense of self and survival that we will drop whatever we are doing whenever they arise.

Have you ever found yourself in a café, immersed in work, oblivious to the cacophony of dozens of conversations, only to suddenly perk up as you catch your name spoken faintly across the room? This is known as the cocktail party effect—it's your attentional filter functioning as intended, identifying things that are important and bringing them to your attention so you become consciously aware of them.

Incredibly, recent research from the University of Chicago shows that due to their intimate and continuous presence in our lives, our smartphones have rocketed to the very top of this hierarchical tree of importance, receiving privileged attentional space on par with our own names. This is unprecedented. In the study, participants were placed under three conditions:

1. Devices placed nearby and in sight, face down on their desks.
2. Devices placed nearby but out of sight, in their pocket or bag.
3. Devices placed in a separate room altogether.

The participants were then given puzzles and other tasks that tested their working memory and intelligence. Their results indicated that the mere presence of their smartphone (regardless of whether the smartphone was on their desk or out of sight inside their pocket) reduced cognitive capacity. Whether concealed or staring back at you, your phone disrupts your ability to focus on a task.

Imagine how hard it would be to concentrate on anything if there were someone next to you at all times, constantly shouting your name. As far as your attentional filters are concerned, this is exactly what your phone is doing! If you always have your phone with you, a certain amount of attention is always being given to it. This magical shouting device is also the most popular consumer product ever made; nearly everyone in the developed world—even children—owns one and carries it with them everywhere. No wonder we've seemingly lost our ability to pay attention—we're all being inundated with the beautiful but slightly alarming sound of our names being shouted at us every second of the day.

What is truly fascinating about the University of Chicago experiment, though, is that when the participants were asked if they were *thinking* about their phones during the task, they reported "not at all" most of the time. So, the fact that their cognitive capacity was directly impaired by the proximity of their phones means this is something we can't necessarily "feel" in our awareness. Simply put, you don't even register that it's happening.

Reinforce Your Attentional Filters With a Sticky Note

Jonathan was experiencing this constant draw of attention to his smartphone, and by applying the M.O.R.E. Method, he began to gain insight into just how automatic and unconscious this process was. While waiting for a bus one day, he suddenly realized that he was scrolling through his Twitter feed before he was consciously aware that he was even holding his phone.

The trouble is that in order to begin to change this habit, he needed to increase his awareness of the process as it happened—and this was no easy task. So, in desperation, he decided to slap a large yellow sticky note on his phone screen. That way, he thought, there is no way he could miss the fact that he's unlocking his phone. He then went one step further and used a Sharpie to write a single word on the sticky note: "Intention". His hope was that not only would he notice that he was trying to unlock his phone but that this word would prompt a question: Could he identify a clear goal or intent for unlocking his device? Or was it just a habitual reflex? Based on the answer, he would then either decide to continue or to put the phone away and return to whatever he had been doing beforehand.

In this experiment, the sticky note supports our attentional filters by externalizing the process and making it explicit and conscious. Jonathan was amazed at how powerful a sticky note could be in giving him agency over his attention, helping him feel more in control of where he was placing his focus.

As you continue to practice paying attention, we strongly encourage you to give this a go. You can try mixing it up with different words on your sticky note or even different objects on your device (e.g., a rubber band).

Strengthening Attention With the Muscle of Mindfulness

The great psychology pioneer William James described attention training as the "very root of judgment, character, and will." While the science of attention has grown into a sophisticated field of research, the boldness of this claim still holds water. What we pay attention to, and how, shapes our inner world—and over time, it also shapes our brains and our whole reality. As artist and author Jenny Odell writes in *How to Do Nothing*, "patterns of attention— what we choose to notice and what we do not—are how we render reality for ourselves."

But what exactly does attention training entail? Does it mean training our attention to stay in one place? Not exactly. William James originally described it as "the faculty of bringing back a wandering attention, over and over again." Did you spot the difference? It is safe to assume that attention will inevitably wander, but the training is in how swiftly and consistently we can keep bringing it back to our object of focus. The moment you notice you're distracted, you're not distracted anymore. It's not "if" but "when" you get distracted.

Normally, when we think of mindfulness, we think of concentrating on something—for example, our breath, a candle or a sound. In fact, that is only part of the practice. The other part is learning to notice when the mind gets distracted and bringing it back to your object of meditation. Nothing else is necessary. Even asking, "How on earth did I get distracted?" is just another distraction. The simplicity of mindfulness, of continually bringing your mind back, gradually calms it down.

Mindfulness practice is a particular kind of attention training. It reduces that goal interference we mentioned earlier. Through such seemingly simple exercises, practitioners are gradually empowered to reclaim their attention for their own purposes— training the muscle of the mind to notice when it has strayed from its chosen object and to return to the object. And without getting too meta here, learning to pay attention to attention itself is how we will understand attention's habitual patterns and learn how this may be helping us or failing us.

There are many theories about how exactly the brain changes with mindfulness training. Many researchers have found that the prefrontal cortex actually increases in size and density the more we practice: The working memory in the hippocampus expands, making it easier for us to stay on track. We develop more control—executive control—enabling us to implement more of those top-down goals without getting distracted.

The evidence is compelling—a comprehensive review of 23 studies highlights that individuals engaging in mindfulness training for just a few months exhibit improved performance in tasks testing their ability to dismiss distractions. Long-term practice has been found to not only enhance current focus but also serve as a deterrent to the natural decline in attention control that accompanies aging.

What's amazing is that it is the process of getting distracted and coming back, again and again, to our focal point that is actually building our attentional capacity. Like lifting weights requires gravity to make us stronger, attention requires distraction to make it stronger. Keep that in mind next time you pick up your phone in a moment of distraction—if you notice it happening, you're no longer distracted and you've built some of that mindfulness muscle!

Your Attention Is More Than a Resource, It Could Be Your Greatest Asset

Throughout our exploration of attention, we've largely been talking about it as a resource—something that, when strengthened and directed efficiently, can help us become more productive or less anxious. But we also believe that your attention is far more than simply a resource. It could even be your most precious asset.

Imagine for a moment the entire universe, stretching out over infinite space and time. For any of us individually, this impossibly vast ground of reality is unknowable. And yet, we each have access to some of it: This is your own personal experience, and it's shaped by who you are, when and where you were born. But even this slice of experience is not fully accessible to you—as we explored earlier, it's impossible for your conscious awareness to take in all of the events and information in your surroundings at the same time. You can only attend to one experience at a time: The words on this page, the feeling of your body in your seat, the sound of the world outside the window.

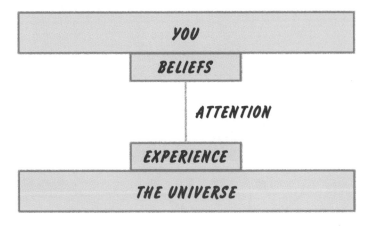

Readers of Liminal Thinking *by Dave Gray may recognize his influence in this image.* Liminal Thinking *is an incredible book about how our beliefs shape everything, and our intention is to build on this understanding in the context of our digital lives.*

Based on what you choose to pay attention to within your experience at any given moment, you then form a set of beliefs about the world. The music you listen to, the books you read, the company you keep and the celebrities you can't stop reading about—all of these sources of input shape your beliefs and therefore your behavior. If you listened to different music, read different books and socialized in different circles, you couldn't help but see the world differently than you do now as a result.

Who you are—the friends you make, the adventures you pursue, the career you choose, the person you marry and the values you uphold—is a result of where you've placed your attention. This means your attention is not simply a resource that makes you more productive, it's a vital link between your experience of reality and your beliefs, making it foundational in shaping the direction and quality of your life. It's the bridge that connects you to the heart of your present experience, moment by moment.

So, what do you want to pay attention to in your life? And do your digital habits currently support you? Use the M.O.R.E. Method to run a few experiments to find out.

Embracing Emotions

Or, How to Debug Your Feelings

The role of emotions in our behavior is so fundamental that it can be easy to take it for granted. For proof, look no further than the well-known neurological case study of a woman who is known simply as "S.M." While walking home through a local park late one night, an unknown man beckoned her toward a bench. Instead of avoiding eye contact and picking up her pace, S.M. walked directly toward him. Terrifyingly, as she got near, the man pulled her close and held a knife against her throat. However, throughout this whole experience, S.M. displayed no fear. She later said that she didn't feel afraid at all. It turns out this was due to a rare brain injury that caused S.M. to be entirely incapable of experiencing fear.

While the idea of being literally fearless may sound like a superpower, the more you hear about S.M's life, the more you realize her inability to feel fear—and therefore assess threats—is a curse. In fact, as a direct result, she's suffered an unusually high degree of violence in her life (including being held at gunpoint and almost being killed in a domestic violence incident).

While most of us are, thankfully, not subject to the extreme situations S.M. has found herself in, we all experience a wide range of strong (sometimes very challenging) emotions on a daily basis—many of which we wish didn't exist. As a result, especially in our digital lives, we can go to all sorts of lengths to avoid them. But all emotions in our lives—the good, the bad and the ugly—serve a very real and important purpose. Learning to acknowledge their value and embrace them is a crucial step toward living your best digital life.

Emotions and Digital Habits Feed Each Other

During a typical day, we often find ourselves needing to switch up our emotions. You may want to feel more enthusiastic about an upcoming budget meeting or embrace a deeper sorrow at a funeral. Perhaps you want to be less frustrated when meeting an errant family member or more outraged about something you know in your heart is wrong. The urge to adjust our emotional states is an ordinary, everyday experience. So it's unsurprising that we've all got so many tricks up our sleeves to work with, lean into or regulate our emotions. This practice can take many forms, such as tidying up to feel less overwhelmed, eating another tub of ice cream to soothe a broken heart, taking a long bath to relax or simply knowing when to walk out of a room to remove yourself from a frustrating situation.

There is one large subset of regulation strategies, which could be described as a redirection, that is now best (or at least most conveniently) done with the help of a digital device. Watching television, listening to music, hanging out with friends, looking at old photos—all of these classic regulation strategies are now done on our smartphones and tablets. It may not be surprising to learn, then, that researchers have found that nearly half of our smartphone use is driven by the need to regulate our emotions— so much so that the smartphone has started to provide levels of personal comfort equivalent to being at home in terms of a place we can go to feel calm and settled.

MOBILIZE

*"You are not your emotions;
you feel your emotions."*
—Michael Singer

1. Clarify Your Intention

Take a moment to consider how your relationship with tech impacts your ability to manage your emotions. Then imagine how you would like this to change—this could be something quite specific, or a broader aspiration for yourself, such as, "I am the kind of person who regulates my emotions in an intentional way, not automatically defaulting to tech."

2. Identify a Moment

Some examples to get you started:
- Opening Instagram on your phone
- Seeing someone post about their success
- Commuting home from work
- Watching YouTube in bed

3. Define Your Ritual

As an example, whenever you start your commute, take a minute to observe your emotions. Make a mental note of any feelings of exhaustion, frustration or anxiety and give them space with the gentle aspiration that you may be free of them.

4. Practice Your Ritual

Throughout the day, keep an eye out for your cue to practice your ritual and use this moment to link your intention to your present situation.

SEE PG. 73 FOR MORE ON HOW TO MOBILIZE

Tech companies, in their pursuit of our time and attention, have made the process of using our devices in this way as frictionless as possible. We usually pick up our devices subconsciously in an attempt to manage our feelings. But as with everything in our digital lives, using tech habitually in this way only serves us if we are aware of and intentional with these habits. As University of Melbourne researcher Dr. Greg Wadley says, "If you're annoyed that your bus is running 5 minutes late so you play *Candy Crush*, that's not hurting anyone and it's better than getting upset." However, he adds, "If you're playing games for 5 hours the night before an exam because you can't get that intense anxiety out of your head—that's not so good."

One of the reasons using tech to regulate emotions can be less than ideal is that online platforms are volatile places. Watching a funny video or texting a friend might take the edge off feelings of unhappiness or loneliness, but much of what we see on our phones can provoke and feed the very feelings we're trying to avoid. During the COVID years, many of us would actively look up information about the virus to quell the feeling of uncertainty and lack of control, but what we'd find would often be more distressing. Researchers such as Professor Wally Smith, who studies computer-human interaction, call this "disrupted regulation."

The situation is even worse when algorithms are designed to provoke or incite emotions like fear or anger rather than help us regulate them. As AI models become more skilled at identifying our moods and emotional patterns, they can use that information for many different purposes. For example, they can tailor your feed with content that will strengthen the very feelings you are trying to reduce—even if those feelings are anxiety, depression or curiosity about self-harm and even suicide. Research on teenagers has found how easy it is for emotions to be reinforced or exacerbated through social media use. When it comes to the attention economy, keeping you online and seeing more ads is more profitable than helping you feel better.

In order to live your best digital life, beginning to unpick this entangled relationship of digital habits and emotions is essential—and it begins with understanding what emotions are in the first place.

Emotions Are Information

Our emotions (and, to a degree, other people's emotions) shape our lives: from happiness to sadness, fear, disgust, anger, surprise and love—the list is long, the influences myriad. But what are emotions, really? Where do they come from?

While much of the nuance is still debated (e.g., the exact number of universal primary emotions), it is widely agreed that emotions have evolved as part of our survival instincts. Since our ancestors faced and overcame recurring challenges, evolution has gifted us access to the emotions that best served them in the form of a nervous system that makes emotional responses immediate, automatic and innate. In other words, emotions are hard-wired evolutionary responses to ancient situations, rapidly providing us with vital information that moves us to act in situations too important to leave to our conceptual thought processes alone.

While these emotions continue to serve us well, the fact that they are rooted in this ancient wiring of our body can often make them seem irrational, leaving us feeling as if there is no discernible logic to something like a sudden onset of jealousy, arousal or irritability. But this is often a case of us receiving the emotional message before we are consciously aware of why we're receiving it or where that message is coming from. This speed of delivery is one of the key advantages of our emotions, giving us a heads up on events we haven't yet processed. But the high speed with which these emotions arrive brings its own problems, making it easy for us to jump to conclusions and react reflexively in ways that don't always match the reality of our situation.

It's easy to see, then, that—for better or worse—emotions trigger us to take action. Much of our behavior is influenced by an emotional nudge, whether it's the posts of a social influencer awakening a strong fear of missing out that triggers the purchase of a specific product or a pang of disappointment from a job rejection email that triggers a weekend of binge-watching *The Big Bang Theory*.

In our digital lives, we are constantly rubbing up against our own emotions as well as the emotions of others, which in turn triggers even more emotions in us. If we think of emotions as information, that's a lot of information to receive. Knowing how to respond is therefore essential to our digital lives.

Emotions Are Surprisingly Physical

We may think our emotions arise and play out in the brain, much like in the film *Inside Out*, in which the characters (Joy, Sadness, Fear, Disgust and Anger) are seated in the brain's command center. While this image makes for a convenient storytelling device, it is also a misleading simplification.

In reality, emotions are fundamentally physical. Psychologist William James and physiologist Carl Lange both independently proposed a theory (now known as the James-Lange theory) that suggests our emotions are derived from our bodily reactions. This suggests that we don't tremble because we're afraid—we're afraid *because* we tremble. As we noted in Practice 1, our body posture and movements can change our emotional state, and we can feel happier simply because we're already bringing a smile to our face. It's counterintuitive, sure, but this theory has sparked a revolution in understanding the physiological basis of emotions.

Have you ever wondered why we turn pale when we are scared? Our body redirects blood from our face to our large muscles, like our legs, preparing us for potential flight. At the same time, our body becomes momentarily petrified, giving us a few critical seconds to assess the situation and decide if hiding might be a better option. The brain's emotional centers control this reaction, releasing a flood of hormones that put our

OBSERVE

1. Check In

Begin by taking a few deep breaths. Notice the sensation of your breath as you inhale and exhale. Allow your breath to become slow and natural.

2. Choose Something to Observe

This is an observation practice to help strengthen the skill of emotional self-awareness—labeling your emotions. Begin to shift your attention from your breath and observe what you are currently feeling at this moment in time. Imagine your emotions as a river—it could be a gentle trickle or a raging torrent. Picture yourself standing on the banks of that river simply noticing what is flowing by.

3. Get Curious

Be curious about whatever emotions arise. Acknowledge each one as you become aware of it, giving it a label. "Hello, excitement," "Welcome back, jealousy," "I see you, despair" and so on. Notice how intense each emotion feels and whether it's getting stronger or weaker as you observe it. Some feelings are more like waves or bursts. You could use the wheel of emotions in this chapter (pg. 166) as a support if it feels difficult to find the right label for whatever you are feeling.

4. Keep Coming Back

Allow yourself to feel the emotion fully, label it, then return to your breath. If you feel overwhelmed and swept away by the emotion (whether it's pleasant or unpleasant), return to observing your breath until you feel better, then come back to the labeling practice.

SEE PG. 81 FOR MORE ON HOW TO OBSERVE

body in a state of alertness, ready for action. Our focus becomes more precise, allowing us to evaluate the threat and determine the most appropriate response as quickly as possible.

This flurry of physiological activity demonstrates that emotions prime you at the physical level—you could even say that feeling an emotion can be considered the first step of a physical response. It's important to recognize this because, as we learned earlier, using technology often disconnects us from our bodies. Since emotions have a strong physical basis, working through them will often require some form of physical activity (going for a run to dissipate overexcitement or doing box breathing to calm the nerves). If you're spending hours behind a screen accumulating various emotions, then that lack of motion could leave you feeling very uncomfortable. There's no outlet!

Therefore, when adopting habits for your best emotional digital life, start with the experiments we explored in Practice 1 that help you reconnect with and engage your physical body.

Digital Emotional Intelligence

While the information and experiences these various feelings and moods generate can be a lot to handle, the good news is we are not completely adrift and rudderless on the sea of our emotions. Thanks to our executive function (the intentional part of our brains), once an emotion has arisen, we have the ability to recognize it, regulate it and then choose what to do next. Imagine anger arising as you read a spicy headline in your news feed—at that moment, there is a risk you'll enter a doom-loop of emotional responses (such as feeling angry about the fact that you are angry), which can then spiral endlessly. But your executive function allows you to pause and make a different choice: to reassess and take a path of de-escalation through reasoning and action.

This kind of response requires a set of core skills that, thankfully, we can actively train our minds to embrace. Psychologist Daniel Goleman famously coined the term "Emotional Intelligence" (aka

EQ) to describe these skills collectively. Of these skills, Goleman specifically identifies two that are particularly useful when we are first trying to embrace and work with our emotions in our digital lives: self-awareness and self-regulation.

Why are these two so important? First, if you lack awareness of what you feel from moment to moment, then it's difficult to do anything with your emotions other than be swept away by them. Self-awareness helps you notice emotions as they play out in your body, which in turn creates the opportunity for you to begin intentionally changing them, which is self-regulation.

We will now take some time to explore both of these skills— emotional self-awareness and self-regulation—in more detail and consider how we can apply the M.O.R.E. Method to start to develop a form of digital emotional intelligence.

Self-Awareness Gives Space to Your Emotions

Self-awareness, in short, means being aware of both your mood and your thoughts about that mood, as explained by John Mayer, an American psychologist who co-developed a popular model of emotional intelligence along with Yale professor Peter Salovey.

How can you bring this about? Begin by focusing on what you are feeling and allow your attention to welcome whatever passes through your awareness with impartiality, like a curious but uninvolved observer. If you consider your emotions to be like a river, this self-awareness has you standing on the riverbank, not being swept up or away by the emotions and therefore able to see them clearly.

The reality isn't always this elegant. If you are feeling overwhelmed by uncomfortable emotions, self-awareness could also simply be the repeated thought, "I wish I didn't feel this way." This still counts—after all, you need to be able to be aware that you feel uncomfortable in order for this thought to arise.

If none of this comes easily, don't worry—some of us are more naturally attuned to notice our emotions. Many emotions play out on an unconscious level and don't always cross over into our awareness. That doesn't mean you can't get better at noticing them, however. Self-awareness is a muscle that is essential for living your best digital life, and research has shown it's possible to strengthen that muscle. One key obstacle is getting caught up in the emotions you are trying to observe, which can happen for two main reasons:

1. **Stickiness.** We're so entangled in our emotions that we usually can't see them (like a fish doesn't perceive the water around it). Emotions also feel like a command you have to obey or a rule you have to follow. In psychology lingo, this is sometimes referred to as "cognitive fusion."

2. **Avoidance.** We feel so uncomfortable with our emotions that we prefer to push them away. The stronger our tolerance for being able to sit with emotions, the more clearly we can see them.

To overcome both these challenges, we need to take a big step back. Big enough that we can observe our emotional landscape clearly, but not so big that we're running out the back door! It's a bit like choosing a seat at the theater: We want to be able to view all the actors well enough to take in the whole atmosphere, but we also don't want to squint to make out the expressions on their faces.

Name How You're Feeling

How do we create the distance required to become emotionally self-aware? Anything that grounds us in our bodies can help us see what is going on with greater clarity. Slowing down and taking deep breaths. Using words to try to describe what we are aware of can also put us in observation mode, a position of

REFLECT

1. Warm Up

Spend a couple of minutes using the observe technique to watch an object (or practice some box breathing) to settle your mind and focus it, ready for reflection.

2. Reflect

Now swap out the object you were focusing on in the warm-up (e.g., your breath, an object, a sound) and focus on a question, for example:

How do I use my devices to manage my emotions?

- Which app(s) do I use to cheer myself up?
- Which app(s) do I use when I'm feeling stuck?
- Which app(s) do I use when I'm feeling lonely?
- Are there certain apps I'm overusing to manage my emotions?
- Which emotions am I struggling with the most these days?

3. Digest

Wherever your reflection ends up, notice the atmosphere left in your mind: Is it one of clarity, confusion or exhaustion? Whatever the case, simply pay attention to that feeling and let this experience seep into your being for a few moments before carrying on with your day.

4. Make It Your Own

Try reflecting on things that particularly inspire or intrigue you—here are a few more suggestions to get you started:

- If I'm shopping online as a form of retail therapy, what is the cost over the course of a year?
- When I use a particular app to feel more connected to friends, how long does that good feeling last?

SEE PG. 89 FOR MORE ON HOW TO REFLECT

curiosity rather than stickiness or avoidance. Even though the English language alone has about 3,000 possible words to describe nuanced emotions (such as annoyed, bitter, frustrated, fuming, livid, irate), few of us use more than a dozen or so (angry, very angry, incredibly angry). As a result, noticing different emotions can be tricky if we are unable to find the right words.

One simple but powerful tool that can help with this is an emotion wheel. It could be that you are experiencing a very nuanced emotion, such as "embarrassed," but you are unaware that this is rooted in the base emotion of anger. Or perhaps you know you are sad, but you lack the emotional vocabulary to specifically identify that sadness as powerlessness or vulnerability.

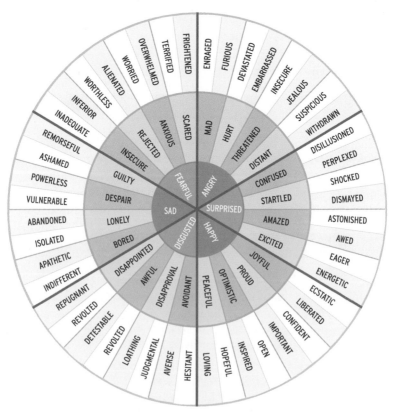

Once you can name your feelings more easily, you can begin to reap the benefits in your digital life. Next time you're scrolling LinkedIn seeing your friends and colleagues humblebrag about their achievements, consider whether you feel any resistance to feeling happy for them. You may even be hitting the "celebrate" button or typing out "Congrats!" But what emotions are you really feeling? In our experience, it's often a form of jealousy. In her book *The Artist's Way*, artist and author Julia Cameron argues that even jealousy can provide us with useful information: "Jealousy is always a mask for fear: fear that we aren't able to get what we want; frustration that somebody else seems to be getting what is rightfully ours even if we are too frightened to reach for it."

Accurately decoding an emotion, especially jealousy, can help you learn more about yourself if you put in the work to explore the feeling. As an exercise, make a list of five people you're jealous of and look them up online. Ask yourself, "What am I jealous of about this person?" Get specific. Maybe they seem to travel a lot for work. Maybe they seem to have a great team. Maybe they have a fantastic wardrobe! Or maybe they just seem at peace with themselves. Write it all down, then move on to the next person. Once you've finished, you'll have a long, envy-inducing list. Now, look for patterns. Note what trends arise (the pattern might even surprise you!), then decide what active steps you can take to shape your life in that direction. Turn your jealousy into clarity, courage and commitment to going after what you really want.

The Most Notorious Emotion in Digital Life: Boredom

When increasing your self-awareness of your emotions in your digital life, there is one emotion that experience has shown won't take long to rear its head: boredom. But what is boredom? Is it even an emotion? There's a lot of debate in psychology about this, but the growing consensus is that yes, it is an emotion like any other. Boredom is defined as the feeling of not being able to engage meaningfully in whatever it is you're doing. This is why you could be in a colorful, exciting place—say, Disney World or a bustling marketplace—and still feel utterly bored. It's not about the intensity or amount of stimuli around you but whether or not you feel stimulated. It's a measure of how satisfied you are with your engagement in the world. Leo Tolstoy described boredom as "the desire for desires." We want to act in a way that springs from our desires, we want to be doing something—just not any option currently available to us.

From a digital habits perspective, boredom is a critical emotion to embrace. If you reflect on it, you may not be able to remember the last time you were truly bored. Many of us may recall having to cope with stretches of boredom as kids (especially if you were born before 2007 when the iPhone was invented), but less so now. We are so used to having tablets and smartphones at our fingertips to distract, entertain and soothe us that many of us no longer know how to be bored. But when boredom does strike and there is no immediate distraction at hand (e.g., the flight has no free Wi-Fi or the doctor's office lacks appealing magazines), recent studies have shown that people start to behave in strange ways. In one study, participants voluntarily gave themselves electric shocks rather than sitting in solitude for as little as 15 minutes. In another experiment, people were given a (rather morbid) option to shred maggots in a coffee grinder rather than watching a boring video, and 18 percent of people decided to give that a go (but thankfully for the maggots, the machine did not actually have the ability to shred these insects, as the participants were led to believe). In other words, being bored has been shown to take some of us down pretty dark paths of emotional management.

What is the healthier response to boredom? Rather than

Fully Embrace Boredom

When boredom creeps in, try to sit with it without distracting yourself with digital media to see what you find.

Limit News Exposure

Reduce the frequency of news updates to have more control over your emotional states while staying informed about the things that matter.

See Yourself in Others

Observe the digital habits of others as a mirror of yourself—note the emotions that arise in you and reflect on what they are telling you.

Orchestrate JOMO (the Joy of Missing Out)

Identify and schedule activities that bring you contentment without worrying about missing out on what others may or may not be doing.

List Your Triggers

Note emotional triggers as they arise in your digital life. Design ways to reduce each trigger to regulate your emotions.

Practice Emotional Alchemy

When difficult emotions arise, try to see them purely as data points and consider how they could be reframed to your advantage.

Observe a Digital Sabbath

Make time where you avoid specific technologies and observe how it impacts your emotions. This could be once per week, month or year.

Implement a "Low-Sugar" Digital Menu

List self-contained (no infinite scroll) digital activities you can use as a distraction, like Wordle. These are like low-sugar treats.

Use an Emotion Wheel

An emotion wheel can help you identify how you are feeling. Write down your emotions in a journal.

Use Digital Distraction Skillfully

Identify digital activities that give you comfort and relaxation. Learn how to best use them to distract from extreme emotions.

SEE PG. 97 FOR MORE ON HOW TO EXPERIMENT

always picking up our device to end the feeling, we can use this moment of friction to ask ourselves, "What can I use this moment to do instead?" Recently, Menka was beginning her one-hour train journey into central London when she noticed her phone battery was at 5 percent. First, there was the regular phone panic. Once she realized it was fine—nobody really needed to contact her for a while and she knew how to get where she was going—she calmed down and switched it off to conserve the battery for any emergency calls or map-checking she may need later. After spending the first part of the journey peering over to see what other people were doing on their screens, something shifted inside her and she started to explore more. (The leading theory about boredom is that this opening up to options is the very evolutionary purpose of boredom; it nudges us to explore new information in our environments.) Menka noticed she still felt sad about some news headlines she had read in the morning. She noticed her right knee was aching but her left was fine. She noticed a man in a suit carefully holding a box of donuts, clearly taking this task seriously. She noticed her T-shirt was especially soft and comfortable. In this particular situation, the boredom was a catalyst and motivation to notice her surroundings and feelings with a renewed sharpness.

No wonder many artists consider boredom an essential foundation for their creativity. The queen of detective novels, Agatha Christie, said, "There's nothing like boredom to make you write." By staying bored for a period of time, you give yourself more opportunities for creative thoughts and insights—you allow space for your thoughts to seek out novel connections. You give your often harried focus room to take in your surroundings and switch off the autopilot.

As every new technology in your life attempts to be more "frictionless" than the last (maybe it charges itself, or doesn't need to be manually switched on because it's voice-activated or reads your mind), there are fewer and fewer situations in which you might experience boredom. That comes at a cost: By always being engaged in your devices, what are you missing out on?

Regulate Your Emotions by Reframing Them

Once you've spent time increasing your emotional self-awareness, you're in a much better position to regulate your emotions. This means taking action to manage your emotions through many methods, such as increasing desired emotions, decreasing undesired ones, creating space around them or reframing them.

What do we mean by reframing emotions? Imagine you're on a company-wide video call about to announce the new project you've worked on for the past year. The moderator is just about to "spotlight" you and your slides. It's a big moment. You feel fluttery inside your stomach and tight in your shoulders, and now there's no denying that you're nervous. As we learned earlier, this emotion is simply information coming from your body. How you interpret this information will determine how you experience the emotion. If you interpret the information as fear, that can make you feel even more anxious. But if you instead reframe this information as your body being excited about this opportunity, it can be a helpful way to manage the emotion and allow you to give the presentation of your career.

This might sound a bit naive, like something you'd learn on the first day of a Positive Thinking for Beginners course. But there's plenty of evidence to suggest that how you interpret and evaluate any event—including the emotions themselves—plays a huge role in how you feel and how you respond.

Note that reframing an emotion is not about denying an existing emotion and steamrolling it with another. It's simply another interpretation of the information your emotions are delivering to you. Finding the most helpful interpretation for yourself in any given moment is a skillful way of embracing and harnessing your emotions to align with your goals. Going back to those butterflies in your stomach, you can interpret the feeling as fear or excitement, and whichever one you choose shapes your state of mind as you step into presentation mode.

When you notice emotions popping up in your digital life, you can begin to use this process of reframing to help manage them. Lying in bed scrolling through all the feeds at a million miles an hour because you are feeling absolutely wired and overstimulated? Perhaps your emotions are actually telling you that you're completely exhausted and need to go to sleep.

Sometimes the Most Skillful Response Is Distraction

When you're absolutely exhausted or when life feels particularly sticky, managing your emotions can be difficult. In these moments, it's not possible to use the techniques we've discussed like increasing your awareness of emotions, reframing them or even just knuckling down and attempting to ignore them. As a result you will find yourself much more vulnerable to distractions as you seek out ways to divert your attention from the discomfort.

It could be tempting to think this is the time when you need to diligently deploy anti-distraction strategies, like web-blocking apps or noise-canceling headphones. Writer Oliver Burkeman observes that these approaches rely on "denying yourself access to the places you usually go for relief from emotional unpleasantness, but they don't address the unpleasantness itself."

In these moments, distraction can be a great way to skillfully give yourself a break from the strong emotion that isn't serving you, allowing you to return to the difficulty later when you feel calmer and more centered. Walking it off, watching a video, doing a crossword on your phone or calling a friend—these can all be useful methods for regulating emotions. This skillful use of distractions is not about avoidance but rather a purposeful redirection of focus, allowing for a more thoughtful and deliberate approach to managing emotions. In essence, the ability to skillfully navigate distractions becomes a key component in the toolbox for emotional regulation and well-being.

Of course, the danger here is that the distraction becomes a slippery slope into something far less intentional. One video becomes two, and eight sneaky autoplays later, you're headfirst down the rabbit hole. There is no simple solution to this other than regular experimentation using the M.O.R.E. Method to understand how best to apply helpful distraction effectively for yourself. One trick you can apply is to keep a light level of awareness regarding how you feel while you are distracting yourself. Say, for example, you decide to watch a trashy YouTube video—this could be skillful, as it can create a sense of space and ease. At this stage, you could end up zoning out completely (entering the autopilot mode of the intentional habits grid from Principle 3, see pg. 63), which would likely lead to less productive YouTube viewing in a blink. Instead, try to playfully keep a light awareness of how you are feeling while watching the video and note what's happening to your emotional state. If there is no change to the intensity, then continue with videos while still keeping an eye on your emotions. If you notice things beginning to soften and mellow a little, you've reached a good moment to switch away from the videos before things get too mindless.

It turns out that carefully treading this balance is key to embracing all of the emotions in your digital life—holding them in your awareness, while giving them plenty of space at the same time. Your tools of Observation and Reflection will be particularly useful here.

Cultivating Finite Relationships

Or, How to Cultivate Quality Connections

Karen X. Cheng woke up one morning, hit refresh and found that one of her Instagram videos had over a million likes! She was stunned. In her own words, it was the highest high she'd ever felt. A million strangers had just told her that she was talented, special and wanted. Who wouldn't crave that positive connection with others?

Cheng spent the next decade chasing that high. She carved her niche online by making irresistible clips for social media and studying the algorithms intensely. It worked! She has high-fived Mark Zuckerberg in the metaverse. Reese Witherspoon has liked her videos. She has creative industry accolades and awards to show for her success.

But Cheng was also heading toward a depression. Every post and high was soon followed by a crash. So she'd make another post, get another hit of likes, ride another high, another crash...and each high was duller than the last. Soon, she felt empty.

Cheng had fallen into the trap of measuring her social wealth in views and likes rather than respect from herself and those whose opinions she valued. So when a post wouldn't get as many likes as usual, she felt terrible. When it's possible to have infinite friends on the internet "liking" your work, 10 likes feels like nothing. Cheng hasn't quit social media (her online fame is how she makes her living!), but she's changed her relationship with the attention she receives to protect her mental health.

While this trajectory of events is fairly predictable, nobody has told the kids. Ask a hundred children what they want to be when they grow up and social media influencer will be at the top of the list. A 2021 poll showed that "YouTube star" was the number one coveted job, more than doctor, athlete or firefighter. This is not just a one-off result. Another study, conducted in 2019 on behalf of Lego, found that children in the U.K., U.S. and China are three times more likely to want to become a YouTuber than an astronaut.

We need a new narrative about what it means to be loved and appreciated in our digital lives, one that places less emphasis on infinite weak interactions (likes and subscribes) and more emphasis on finite meaningful relationships.

What Makes a Relationship Meaningful?

We all know humans are social creatures. Our drive to connect with others and form relationships is not a whim but a basic need, as important as food, water and shelter.

MORE

MOBILIZE

"Friends are those rare people who ask how we are and then wait to hear the answer."

—Ed Cunningham

1. Clarify Your Intention

Take a moment to consider how your digital habits shape the quality of your relationships. Imagine how you would like this to change—this could be something quite specific or a broader aspiration for yourself, such as, "I'm the kind of person who has meaningful relationships in my digital life."

2. Identify a Moment

Some examples to get you started.

- Opening Facebook
- Observing a couple lost in their devices (and not each other)
- Sitting down for dinner with others
- Getting onto a train or bus

3. Define Your Ritual

As an example—whenever you sit down to eat with others, take a moment to acknowledge their physical presence and what you value about them. Then make a mental resolution to ensure your digital habits support deepening your connection with these people.

4. Practice Your Ritual

Throughout the day, keep an eye out for your cue to practice your ritual and use this moment to link your intention to your present situation.

SEE PG. 73 FOR MORE ON HOW TO MOBILIZE

In fact, multiple studies have shown our happiness, health and susceptibility to disease are influenced by our connection to others. One such study found that when assessing if a heart attack victim would survive over the 12 months following their injury, the biggest predictor (surpassing exercise, obesity and alcohol consumption!) was the quality and number of relationships they had. A "quality relationship" is one that leaves you feeling supported, loved and valued—not just with friends and family but also colleagues, neighbors and pets! But meaning doesn't happen by accident. It arises from a cocktail of shared experience, mutual trust and care.

These qualities need to be demonstrated consistently over time, in words and deeds. No matter how good our intentions are, if people are unable to experience them, then it's hard for a meaningful relationship to develop. This is essentially the experience of the 23 percent of people who say being "phubbed" (snubbed in favor of a mobile phone) by their partners is a problem in their relationship. Therefore, whether it's through spoken or non-verbal body language, good communication is essential to demonstrating and satisfying our fundamental need for connection.

Using the M.O.R.E. Method to nurture the relationships in your digital life means experimenting to discover which intentional habits help you communicate, empathize and build trust. Thankfully, we now have myriad options since the ways in which we can connect with others is almost unlimited.

Your Infinite Potential for Connection

When the first transatlantic undersea cables formed direct lines of communication between Europe and Canada in 1854, the world became significantly smaller overnight.

Sure, telegrams were sent in Morse code at a glacial 0.1 words per minute, but these cables laid the foundation for internet cables that would facilitate direct, instantaneous connections between almost any two points on the planet imaginable. Today, even people in the few remaining disconnected corners of the globe can't avoid participating in this vast network thanks to the rapid deployment of satellites that transcend any last remaining barriers.

It goes without saying that this technology is powerful for helping sustain your most valued connections. Even if your closest friend moves to a different continent, both of you can easily pick up your conversations right where you left off. As a result, the gap between thinking of someone and communicating with them is astonishingly small—whether you personally know them or not. It's wild to think you could watch an inspiring video from a stranger on the other side of the world, reach out to make a connection and then have a live virtual call with them—potentially all within the same day. But communicating with someone isn't the same as connecting with them. And a meaningful relationship requires connection—whether you're speaking face-to-face or using Morse code.

Your Finite Capacity for Relationships

Considering that our digital tools shape our behavior, this infinite potential for connection is—sadly—setting us up for a fall. The hard truth is that due to our human limitations, we are not capable of continually increasing the number of meaningful relationships in our lives. In fact, British biological anthropologist Robin Dunbar has spent years studying this idea, and his research suggests there is a precise number for the natural limit of meaningful social relationships an individual can manage at any one time:

150. The accuracy and impact of this insight has led to this being referred to as Dunbar's number.

This number is derived as a calculation based on our human limitations, and, more specifically, our brain size. By studying primates' behavior and noting their brain size in relation to their social networks, Dunbar created a model to calculate the limits of their abilities to maintain social networks. This is based on the fact that maintaining social connections requires not just time but also a lot of memory and mental processing ability. He used this model to predict the limit for humans and came up with 148. In the years since, many studies have shown it to be 155 (rounded down to 150 for simplicity). The number 150 (it does vary slightly between individuals) has been shown to hold true across face-to-face networks, active social media connections, wedding parties, village societies, hunter-gatherer tribes and the typical size of the base unit in all modern armies.

Now, you may have already wondered what this means in light of the hundreds if not thousands of connections you have online. This is exactly what Rick Lax, journalist at *Wired*, was thinking when he set out to disprove Dunbar's number by contacting each of his 2,000 Facebook friends with a personal message, working through them in alphabetical order. In doing so, he found that many of the "friends" he was reaching out to had gotten married, moved away, lost a parent or experienced some other major life event that he was hearing about for the first time. He soon realized he didn't know what to say to most of them. By the end of the experiment, Lax felt a clarity and appreciation for those he considered his true friends, a number much lower than 150.

If you think 150 feels small, then it gets even more eye-opening when you understand that there are layers of intimacy within that number. Dunbar has identified five

OBSERVE

1. Check In

Begin by taking a few deep breaths. Notice the sensation of your breath as you inhale and exhale. Allow your breath to become slow and natural.

2. Choose Something to Observe

This is an observation practice to try out when using social media—paying attention to your feed. Shift your attention from your breath and observe what you see on your feed. Notice the colors, images and text as well as the thoughts and emotions that arise in response as you scroll.

3. Get Curious

Be curious about every aspect of the experience, as if this were the first time you have ever used social media. How do you feel as you open the app? Do you have a desire to connect or disconnect? How does it feel to scroll through the feed? What emotions arise? If a particular piece of content draws your eye, be curious about that. What is it that caught your attention? How are you reacting to it?

4. Keep Coming Back

Social media feeds are busy places, so distraction will always be just around the corner when you practice this. Move slowly, scrolling with your fingers and your mind at a snail's pace. When distraction inevitably arises and you notice that you've lost the thread of the practice, drop whatever thoughts arose and bring your attention back to your feed.

SEE PG. 81 FOR MORE ON HOW TO OBSERVE

people as the limit of close friends (people who would not hesitate to drop everything to support or help you) we are capable of having. In addition, he identified 15 as the maximum number of best friends (the people you socialize with most regularly and with whom you exchange mutual favors) we can manage—and that number includes the five best friends as well as immediate family. Incredibly, maintaining these 15 best friendships demands 60 percent of our social time. These are the "finite relationships" we are talking about. For this reason, we should be intentional about who those people are.

Despite Being Hyperconnected, Loneliness Is on the Rise

Despite most of us having far more than 150 connections online, loneliness is more pervasive than ever. U.S. Surgeon General Vivek Murthy has been ringing the warning bell about a "loneliness epidemic" even before the COVID-19 pandemic, and since then, things have only gotten worse. And it's not just older people as one might expect, it's young people too. A 2018 survey in the U.K. by the Prince's Trust found that 35 percent of young people say they have never felt more alone. According to another survey by the BBC's Loneliness Experiment that spoke to over 55,000 people, 40 percent of young people (ages 16 to 24) felt lonely compared to 27 percent of people over 75.

Loneliness is not just a wishy-washy feeling. In Practice 3, we looked at how every emotion has an evolutionary basis (pg. 159) and how emotions are not just mental but also physical phenomena. Loneliness can be seen as a vital warning signal (like hunger and thirst) that tells us a basic human need is not being met. This signal comes from deep within our brain and is experienced as a craving. A group of researchers used fMRI to demonstrate this by examining the brain activity of people who had undergone 10 hours of social isolation and 10 hours of fasting on separate days. They found that when we're isolated from people, seeing a photo of someone engaging in a social activity triggers cravings in our brain similar to the food cravings we may experience after going without food for 10 hours. In other words, people who experience social isolation or loneliness crave social connection like a hungry person craves food.

The most common way to satisfy this social craving these days is not by going to the club or bar but by engaging with social media. Celebrities create connections with us by speaking to us conversationally, letting us know about their personal lives, revealing bits of information that are framed as vulnerabilities. The content is often shared in domestic settings: in bedrooms, among family and friends, informal and unpredictable, like real friends or extended family. We often watch or listen alone, and in those moments, it's easy to think they are speaking directly to us. But these influencers don't check all the "true friend" boxes we mentioned earlier—sure, you might empathize with them when they playfully rant about their spouse or sibling, and the more you return to their content, the more you might enjoy these carefully curated peeks into their lives. But do you truly feel a sense of mutual obligation with them? Can you? Should you?

Meanwhile, the opportunity cost is unmistakable. To be clear, we all sometimes find joy in watching and commenting on a stranger's Instagram story—on some days, it might be your favorite thing to do. That's OK. But it's good to apply the M.O.R.E. Method to observe how often this happens and reflect on what value it brings versus the potential lost opportunities to invest this time in your most meaningful relationships.

Clarify Your Intention for Social Media

By now, we have hopefully convinced you that more connections don't automatically equate to a better digital life. And yet, like a hotel buffet, we often default to an all-you-can-eat approach to our social media connections. When eating, it's easy to overindulge because our brains rely on cues to know when we are full, including hormone release and visual clues, such as an empty bowl. Remove these cues and you can alter behavior. One study titled "Bottomless Bowls" demonstrated this by having some participants unknowingly eat from self-refilling bowls while others received normal bowls. Those with bottomless bowls inadvertently consumed 73 percent more. Even when confronted with the data, they didn't believe it! Nor did they perceive themselves as more sated than those eating from normal bowls.

Social media is its own bottomless bowl. The companies behind sites like YouTube, Instagram and TikTok have removed the visual cues that make us conscious of how much we consume, serving us a glut of content in the form of an infinitely scrolling page. And it really is infinite. In 2022, 2.45 billion pieces of content were created on Facebook on a daily basis. That's a lot of soup and very little satisfaction. In fact, Aza Raskin (the inventor of infinite scroll) estimates that—at the very minimum—his creation wastes the equivalent of 200,000 human lifetimes per day through unintended social media use. He is on record as saying he regrets creating it and has co-founded a nonprofit organization to try to undo some of the damage it's done disconnecting us from what matters.

What's particularly unhelpful about this way of engaging with social media is that it quickly becomes unconscious and passive. In this mode, we scroll not to connect but rather to avoid the somehow painful idea of stopping the act of scrolling altogether. We tend not to stop and engage with

REFLECT

1. Warm Up

Spend a couple of minutes using the Observe technique to watch an object (or practice some box breathing) to settle your mind and focus it, ready for reflection.

2. Reflect

Now swap out the object you were focusing on in the warm-up (e.g., your breath, an object, a sound) and, in its place, focus on a question, for example:

Do I believe there is value in practicing finite relationships?

- Do I have more than 15 best friends?
- Am I able to give them all the attention they deserve?
- What would happen if I increased that number?
- What would happen if I decreased that number?

3. Digest

Wherever your reflection ends up, notice the atmosphere left in your mind: Is it one of clarity, confusion or exhaustion? Whatever the case, simply pay attention to that feeling and let this experience seep into your being for a few moments before carrying on with your day.

4. Make It Your Own

Try reflecting on things that particularly inspire or intrigue you. Here are a few more suggestions to get you started:

- How much of my online time do I invest in meaningful relationships?
- Where do I most need to set boundaries in my digital communication?
- Which of my relationships works best in the digital world?

SEE PG. 89 FOR MORE ON HOW TO REFLECT

what we are seeing in a meaningful way—instead, we pause just long enough to get a quick emotional hit (joy, disgust, jealousy, indifference) then move on to the next post.

Needless to say, this doesn't do much to foster a sense of meaning in our digital relationships. One experiment that is great for flipping this dynamic on its head is to become more intentional and active with your social media use and practice what author and prolific tweeter @visakanv (Visakan Veerasamy) calls "good reply game." Veerasamy introduces the idea this way: "Every 'utterance' (status, tweet, whatever) is a bit of an invitation, a bit of a proposal. 'Let's play this game.' When strangers read the proposal accurately, and support the game, a shared understanding develops. You can make friends this way." At its heart, good reply game is the art of replying in a way that supports the original poster or speaker by following the "Yes, and..." rule of improv comedy: If someone proposes a scenario, others in the group should accept what the improviser has stated ("Yes") and then expand on that line of thinking ("and..."). This approach can transform your social feeds from endless time-wasters into greenhouses for meaningful connections.

One helpful resource for engaging in good reply game is to take inspiration from conversational maxims by British philosopher H. Paul Grice, which aim to explain how people achieve effective communication in everyday situations:

- **The maxim of quantity**, where one tries to be as informative as one possibly can, giving only what information as is needed and no more.
- **The maxim of quality**, where one tries to be truthful, and does not give information that is false or unsupported by evidence.
- **The maxim of relation**, where one tries to be relevant by saying things that are pertinent to the discussion.

- **The maxim of manner**, when one tries to be clear and concise in what one says, avoiding obscurity and ambiguity.

Experiment with these in your active social media use and observe the impact on your digital relationships.

Finite Relationships Require Setting Boundaries

There are a lot of people in the world. That means practicing finite relationships, by definition, involves saying no to most of them. This is the most extreme form of boundary-setting—intentionally excluding people from your social circle, either for a specific event or in general. While the idea of this can feel harsh and uncaring, it is actually quite the opposite. As Priya Parker, author of *The Art of Gathering*, says, "If everyone is invited, no one is invited…. By closing the door, you create the room." Saying no to some people is what allows us to say yes to others. Since we are experimenting with saying a big yes to the most important people in our lives, saying no to many people will happen either way. Make sure you're doing it with intention rather than by default.

Not all boundaries are that extreme, though—many of them can be set within our meaningful relationships in order to build trust and support by clearly communicating what is acceptable and what is not. When doing this in your digital life, it's crucial to know the difference between a boundary and an imposition. A boundary is a personal statement of what you're not willing to do (e.g., "I am not able to reply to emails between 9 p.m. and 6 a.m."). An imposition, on the other hand, attempts to control someone else's behavior (e.g., "You may not email me between 9 p.m. and 6 a.m.").

Creating a culture in which everyone's needs are met is

ideal, but sometimes prioritizing our own needs means setting a boundary. In this process of balancing needs, boundary expert Dr. Brené Brown notes it's easy to confuse our needs with the strategies we use to meet them. For instance, disregarding emails, even urgent ones, can seem tone-deaf or uncooperative. Jonathan's approach, stating in his email signature that he checks emails only twice a day but is open to urgent phone calls, respects both his own boundaries and the contextual needs of others.

Perhaps the best thing about using boundaries to say "No" more often is that it allows for a more joyful "Yes" when it counts. Implementing device-free times into your schedule, like the old "No phones at the dinner table" rule that many of us have tried, can make it more fun to pick up the phone after you've done the dishes. As author Ryan Holiday puts it: "Less commitments, less drama, less busyness, less screen time. Just less. Part of the reason I want less is so I have room for more. More stillness. More presence."

Finite Doesn't Mean Convenient

You might think that having a handful of intimate relationships in your life—compared to trying to maintain hundreds or thousands of shallower relationships online—is easy. But this is not the case. In the digital age, building meaningful relationships is harder: your most intimate relationship must now also compete with your entertainment device. We have a convenient, frictionless exit route from nearly every interaction. Each time someone fails to captivate us—face-to-face or via online chat—the moment our attention wanes, we can switch to another profile, another site, another conversation. The expectation that a person must be perpetually more engaging than the entire World Wide Web is not only unrealistic but also detrimental to forming deep, meaningful connections.

EXPERIMENT

Broadcast Your Own Terms
Create simple ways of regularly letting others know what your expectations are regarding communication and availability.

Make Your Email Signature Work Harder
Design an email signature that clearly states your own expectations concerning email usage and sets healthy boundaries.

Put Arriving on the Agenda
Build in five minutes at the start of a meeting to formally arrive, giving people the space they need to make sure they can bring their full self.

Practice Good Reply Game
Intentionally take the effort to reply to social posts in a way that constructively adds and builds upon what others share.

Define Pop-Up Rules
As a host, define boundaries for your guests (e.g., keep phones face down on the table, only sharing links to humorous content).

Show Others You Are Busy
Use both physical (e.g., close the door) and digital (e.g., status update) signals to indicate to others that you are not currently available.

Turn Your Volume Up In Meetings
Reduce opportunities for people to hide behind their devices by giving permission for those expecting messages to turn up their volume.

Don't Reply Immediately
Don't reply to every incoming message immediately (unless absolutely necessary). Instead, come back to it when you are ready.

Curate Your Media Feeds
Curate the people on your timelines by removing anyone that is no longer bringing you value and adding others that do.

Tell Others What You Are Doing
When around others, communicate what you are using your phone for so they know why you are focusing on it instead of them.

SEE PG. 97 FOR MORE ON HOW TO EXPERIMENT

The extreme characterization of this is that people are increasingly choosing the easy company of AI over human beings. Siri doesn't complain about our taste in music; Alexa doesn't get passive-aggressive with us for forgetting to buy bread. We don't have to relinquish control in order to be in that relationship. Having intimate relationships with AI agents isn't the stuff of science fiction anymore. The real-life companion AIs such as those offered by the company Replika create such strong ties with their customers that when Replika steered the AI away from erotic roleplay, customers who had come to depend on it were distraught.

We are drawn to AI that is always "there," operating on our terms, devoid of the complexities and demands (read: chaos) of human relationships. You won't hurt your AI's feelings if you misunderstand them or crack a joke they take the wrong way. You never have to say "I'm sorry" to your AI or the influencers you follow. You move on like nothing happened, an anonymous avatar in a stream of anonymous avatars. Yet this is where the trade-off lies. Putting yourself out there and embracing vulnerability is the price for cultivating authentic relationships. We would argue that the messiness of meaningful relationships is an inconvenience worth leaning into.

Finite Doesn't Mean Static

Now, we're going to suggest something that might sound like the opposite of everything recommended so far: Try making friends with some new people! Wait—there's a good reason.

In our digital lives, boundaries are often set not by us but by algorithms. Designed to show us the most relevant content based on our past interactions, these algorithms create what we know as "filter bubbles." In the early days of the internet, searches and social feeds were straightforward, showing information in reverse chronological order. However, as algorithms evolved to offer more "relevance," they began to shape our digital experiences into echo chambers of familiarity.

There's a significant trade-off here: the comfort of familiarity versus the challenge of encountering new ideas and perspectives. While it's less prickly to stay within the confines of our usual circles, it's essential to step beyond them. This requires a tolerance for inconvenience and discomfort that doesn't come to us naturally (see Principle 2).

A practical way to break out of these echo chambers is to deliberately follow content we wouldn't normally choose. Make the effort to visit sites or hang out in places you normally wouldn't—perhaps an unfamiliar subreddit, an unusual Instagram account or even an alternative search engine. Equally, try making a habit of asking people you meet to recommend their favorite esoteric corner of the web. The aim is to find the modern equivalent of walking in someone else's shoes—engaging in a diverse range of human experiences and viewpoints to challenge our comfort zones and broaden our understanding of the world. By choosing to do this, even when it's uncomfortable, we open ourselves up to growth and empathy in an increasingly polarized digital age.

As with all the human limitations we've described so far (e.g., a body that needs to breathe and emotions that are not always convenient), this should also feel liberating. Embracing our capacity for only a finite number of relationships that can truly be substantive and meaningful enough to support our happiness means that we can be a little more carefree about the number of likes we get on that amazing photo we posted last night.

Who these close people are in our lives will change as we do, as they do and as the seasons do, which is why the M.O.R.E. Method is a practice, not a one-and-done solution. Keep reflecting on the relationships you are investing your time and energy into and consider if these are the right ones to warrant that big "Yes!"

PRACTICE 5

Exercising Choice

Or, Remembering That You Forgot to Choose

A young man was walking through a quiet, dusty village in Africa. Weary from the heat, he took refuge in the shade of a tree. While surveying the dwellings stretched out before him, he noticed an enormous elephant standing behind a small shack. He'd seen plenty of elephants in the wild, but he'd never seen such a large creature kept in captivity before. To his shock, the only thing keeping the giant creature in place, it seemed, was a flimsy excuse for a piece of rope that was barely tied off properly.

Baffled, the young man approached the shack, keen to get a better look, when an old man appeared in the doorway. "How does your elephant not escape?" the young man blurted out.

"We got her when she was tiny and we used a similar-size rope to tie her up," the old man said. "At that age, it was easy enough to hold her, despite her efforts to wriggle free. At some point, she gave up trying to escape. Even though it's been years since she last tried, the old girl still believes the rope can hold her, so she never tries to break free."

You might recognize this as the ancient parable known as the Elephant Rope. You may not see yourself as an elephant—we all forget things—but you can likely relate to feeling tethered to your digital habits, even though you already possess all the requisite strength to break free.

Tech Teaches Us to Be Helpless

The flimsy ropes in our digital lives can hold us back from reaching our potential. Yet in many cases, all that's stopping us from escaping is a mistaken belief that the rope is too strong to break. This is what is known as learned helplessness: a state in which, as a result of repeatedly experiencing a stressful situation, an individual believes they are unable to control or change their situation, so they stop trying—even when opportunities for change are available. It's easy to recognize when our friends or family members are trapped by this mentality, but we are often blinded by our own circumstances.

Multiple studies demonstrate how learned helplessness plays out in human behavior. In one experiment, groups of people were subjected to an unpleasant noise at a similar high pitch to a baby's cry (a sound virtually no one can ignore) and were instructed to stop the noise by pressing a button in front of them. For Group A, the button ended the sound. For Group B, however, the button did nothing—instead, this group "learned" that their actions had no impact (no wonder "evil scientist" is a common archetype!). Both groups were then asked to solve challenging anagrams

MORE

MOBILIZE

"In every single thing you do, you are choosing a direction.
Your life is a product of choices."
—Dr. Kathleen Hall

1. Clarify Your Intention
Consider how your digital habits shape your sense of autonomy.
Identify one thing you'd like to improve—this could be something
specific or a broader aspiration, such as, "I'm someone who finds
creative ways to make conscious choices in my digital life."

2. Identify a Moment
Here are some examples to get you started:
- Picking a song to play on Spotify
- Sitting down on the sofa after your workday
- Shopping in the supermarket
- Waiting for a bus

3. Define Your Ritual
For example, at the end of your workday, hold your phone without
unlocking it. Mentally acknowledge that the rest of your day will be
shaped by the choices you make when using this device.

4. Practice Your Ritual
Throughout the day, keep an eye out for your cue to practice your ritual
and use this moment to link your intention to your present situation.

SEE PG. 73 FOR MORE ON HOW TO MOBILIZE

while the noise continued. As you might expect, the people in Group A who had the choice to work in peace and quiet outperformed their peers in Group B but, surprisingly, they did so in most cases without pushing the button to stop the noise. Why? It turns out their better performance was due to the *belief* that they had a choice and were in control. Conversely, Group B underperformed because they quickly fell into a condition of learned helplessness. The belief they couldn't do anything about their situation made them passive and reduced their initiative.

Our digital lives are rich with forms of learned helplessness that similarly make us passive, reduce our motivation and diminish our cognitive abilities. We often have experiences that teach us that we can't do much to change our digital habits, so we end up believing we can never change them and live with that gnawing feeling of having no control. Here are some common scenarios that create this sense of digital learned helplessness:

- **Things are always being done for us.** When we constantly outsource tasks to an algorithm (relying on Spotify to pick what we listen to next or Chrome to suggest a list of new articles that it's decided we'd like), we begin to lose touch with our ability to choose or do things for ourselves.
- **Tools are dictated to us.** We all have our preferred apps for doing certain tasks (anything other than Microsoft Teams for communication, ideally!), but often, our employers dictate which tools we have to use, leaving us with no choice but to do things their way.
- **App design nudges our behavior.** When apps keep us hooked (you can't help but check TikTok or your inbox or complete your daily chess puzzle), we feel compelled to engage with our devices, as if we have no choice.

- **We feel like a small cog in a big machine.** Having access to global information (e.g., news apps, Twitter) means being increasingly aware of the world's many challenging macro-events while being left with few options to meaningfully do anything about them.
- **We put blind faith in our tech.** Given the size and resources of tech companies, it's easy to assume their products (both hardware and software) are carefully optimized to perfection, meaning we rarely choose to change their default settings beyond basic things like personalizing our wallpaper! (We'll see later that this is more of a big deal than it may sound).

It can be a bit daunting to consider how tech teaches us to be helpless, but the good news is that we often have more choices in our digital lives than we realize. We've just lost sight of them! By using the M.O.R.E. Method to apply the ideas we'll explore here, it's possible through experimentation to notice where we've developed learned digital helplessness and remember the choices available to us, which can give us back control over our digital lives.

Default Settings Obscure Your Choices

In the early 2000s, Jared Spool, a designer of digital interfaces, wanted to know how people exercised all those choices, controls and settings. He asked users of Microsoft Word to send in their settings files so he could compile a list of the most frequently changed ones. What he found shocked him—less than 5 percent of the users surveyed made any changes at all. Despite the potential choices for optimizing the software, 95 percent of people kept the default settings.

In another twist, the survey also revealed that due to a communication error between the developers at Microsoft, the default settings had actually disabled one of the most helpful features of the program: autosave. If you are of a certain generation, then the keyboard shortcut command + s (or control + s) for saving your files is a deeply ingrained habit (that was likely formed after a painful experience of Word crashing and costing you several hours' worth of hard work). Well, it turns out that for over a decade, there was an option to have Word automatically save your work without having to lift a finger, but hardly anyone benefited from it because, as several participants told Spool, "Microsoft must know what they are doing"—the assumption being it was turned off for a good reason.

If you don't take the time to reflect on the best way to use any given piece of technology, you have instead made the choice of defaulting to whatever habits naturally arise. These default habits could be harmless, but—as we learned from the Microsoft Word incident—it's dangerous to assume things are the best they could be. Living your digital life on default is as much of a choice as living it intentionally, and by establishing your M.O.R.E. practice, you are making the smart choice that will set you up for the best chances of success with your digital habits.

Become a Power User

So much of the popular advice for digital well-being recommends creating boundaries, distancing yourself from tech or abstaining from it altogether. There are undeniable benefits to these approaches, but they are not a complete solution for most people. What they do well is help you find breathing space and top up your depleted inner reserves—like cracking a window to get some fresh air—and help you remember who you are when you're not using your tech 24/7. But this only resets you back to zero—when you resume your normal routine, things can be just as bad. And even when they do

OBSERVE

1. Check In

Begin by taking a few deep breaths. Notice the sensation of your breath as you inhale and exhale. Allow your breath to become slow and natural.

2. Choose Something to Observe

Choose a specific device or app and observe your sense of control while using it. Pay attention to your behavior—be curious about *what* you are doing, and *how* you are doing it. Notice how it *feels*.

3. Get Curious

Being aware of your sense of autonomy can bring up other feelings. If you are feeling in control, there may be a sense of satisfaction or calm. On the other hand, when you are feeling powerless or helpless, it may bring on other feelings, such as apathy or even frustration and anger. It's all good information, so keep an open mind to it all.

4. Keep Coming Back

The moment you notice you've become distracted while observing your feelings, make the choice to return to observing your feeling. This doesn't need to be a heavy-handed choice—it's the momentary recognition of the present and the placing of your attention there once again.

SEE PG. 81 FOR MORE ON HOW TO OBSERVE

leave a lasting impression, this is not a move that you can always go to in the depths of the digital trenches, trying to put out fires in a dicey client situation or run an ad campaign on social media.

What we're going to recommend next is sort of the opposite of a digital detox: developing a sense of mastery over your tech instead. Whether you are editing photos, wrangling numbers in a spreadsheet or writing a manuscript, the app you use will likely offer a plethora of tools, techniques and settings that allow you to customize the way you use it to best fit your needs. That's why—beyond nailing your autosave game—there are plenty of other ways you can (and should) roll up your sleeves and get geeky about your tech.

Think of an experienced pizzaiolo at a restaurant who is able to spin the dough into the air effortlessly, despite being in a challenging environment and working at an unrelenting pace. His complete mastery over the dough gives him a sense of deep calm and satisfaction. By mastering his craft, he gains control over his situation. It's quite rare that we come across the equivalent of this pizza chef in our digital lives, but when we do, it's equally compelling. Power users have all the keyboard shortcuts committed to muscle memory and seem to know all of the esoteric tricks and hacks that allow them to do incredible things with the technology in their hands.

We encourage you to experiment by taking the time to become proficient at using one specific digital technology or skill set—it could be Photoshop, Excel or learning to code or communicate with ChatGPT like a pro. Change all the default settings, make loads of mistakes, watch tutorial videos, learn the keyboard shortcuts. Consider that tech is a tool, and tools can be wielded with mastery. Not only can mastering your tools enable you to realize the results you need in your digital life, it will also leave you feeling in control rather than the other way around.

Hackers are a great example of people who have achieved high levels of mastery over their tech, and, as a result, it's as though tech doesn't present the same limitations for them as it does for ordinary folk. They can access places online that others can't, use tech in creative ways it wasn't originally intended for and fix broken devices most of us would simply throw away.

One story we love that demonstrates how a hacker's mindset can help almost anyone regain control over their tech is about a group of farmers that has been campaigning for "right to repair" legislation. Farmers are naturally self-sufficient, ready to take a wrench to any broken piece of machinery on their land. Yet they have become increasingly irate by "smart" tractors that are built in ways that are impossible to fix. As a result, there are dozens of forums with farmers who have hacked their machines to fix them using unauthorized software. We're not recommending anything illegal, but we do suggest you tinker with your tech and adapt it to serve your goals.

Remember Why You're Using the Tech in the First Place

These days, nearly every digital tech experience is gamified in order to help us get things done. Winning the game in order to get more hearts, subscribers, badges or streaks makes us want to do more, stick with it, keep going. Why? Because games are more fun! This is incredibly useful when it helps us achieve the goals we set. The danger, however, according to experts in the field of motivation, is that we sometimes forget why we're there in the first place.

Take Duolingo: You may have originally decided to learn Spanish in order to feel closer to extended family, but after a 40-day streak, you've lost sight of that choice and now log on purely to keep the streak going. What's happening here is a shift in your underlying motivation—the "why" behind the choices you make. Self-Determination Theory posits that when we do things for our own sense of self-worth and satisfaction (e.g., mastering a language to connect with others), this motivation is described as "intrinsic"—it comes from within. In contrast, "extrinsic" motivation is when we do something primarily to receive a reward defined by others (or from a sense of obligation).

As we've seen, when the juicy carrot of extrinsic motivation is dangled in front of us, it can be a powerful way to help us accomplish difficult tasks. Extrinsic rewards are not inherently bad, of course. But if we are not careful, these rewards can be so powerful that they end up gamifying everything, and we then become motivated almost exclusively by external factors. According to University of Utah philosophy professor C. Thi Nguyen, this slide toward mass gamification happens because "games are more satisfying than ordinary life precisely because their goals are simpler, cleaner and easier to apply."

It's easy to forget when we're using tech that we are abiding by the made-up rules of a game (such as 140 characters only or no hyperlinks in captions). Compared to playing, say, Monopoly, which can last up to 4 or 5 (excruciating) hours, the incentivized nudges to keep posting to social media or take more steps create an essentially infinite game. With the introduction of personalized AI, these nudges will get more intimate, pervasive and compelling. Once you've bought into and internalized the rules, you may not see it as a game at all.

When the majority of your motivation tips into being extrinsic, this is a warning sign and is likely not sustainable. The Duolingo streak works while you are on fire, but when you wake up one day and suddenly realize your life is being dictated by that passive-aggressive little green owl, you can feel resentful and like you have very few choices for

REFLECT

1. Warm Up

Spend a couple of minutes using the observe technique to watch an object (or practice box breathing) to settle your mind and focus it.

2. Reflect

Focus on a question, for example:

- Of all the different forms of tech you use, which ones leave you feeling most helpless, like the elephant in the Elephant Rope story? Which is your weakest link?
- Why do you think that is? How does it actually remove your ability to make your own choices? And why do you keep coming back to it again and again?
- What happens when you remove this piece of tech from your environment for some time?

3. Digest

Wherever your reflection ends up, notice the atmosphere left in your mind: Is it one of clarity, confusion or exhaustion? Whatever the case, simply pay attention to that feeling and let this experience seep into your being for a few moments before carrying on with your day.

4. Make It Your Own

Reframe these questions to make each of them work for you. For example, you might want to ask yourself the opposite question: Which tech leaves you feeling most in control? Why?

SEE PG. 89 FOR MORE ON HOW TO REFLECT

learning your language. A loss of meaning across multiple areas of your life is a recipe for burnout.

It is important to stop playing according to the rules set by the tech, at least from time to time, and to remain connected to your own intrinsic motivations behind using said tech. Remind yourself that your inner reason for getting that smartwatch with the heart rate variability sensor was not just to hit a number but because you want to be more fit.

Tech Drains Your Limited Decisions

Our brains are truly amazing. Every day, each of us processes more than the equivalent of 34 GB of information, and we are able to navigate this complexity by making thousands of decisions over the course of 24 hours. The catch, however, is that there is a biological cost to all this activity. The neurons in the brain are living cells that expend a lot of energy—while the brain takes up only 2 percent of our body weight, it consumes 20 percent of our energy: around 320 calories per day!

Of the brain's many functions, decision-making uses up a high level of energy when compared to activities that can be performed automatically. For example, you may drive home without needing to concentrate hard, allowing you to reflect on a work problem while singing along to a playlist. But as soon as you need to make a unique decision, such as parallel parking into a spot you've never used before, you turn the music down because making the right choices is taxing.

This is why many of us suffer from what is known as decision overwhelm, aka decision fatigue. The majority of decisions we make are (from a zoomed-out perspective) simply not that important: what we wear, which coffee to order, whether to check Twitter or Instagram, whether to delete an email or archive it. Surprisingly, all these little decisions take up the same amount of energy as big ones.

Decision fatigue comes with serious consequences, not in the least that it can cause us to make bad choices. A study from Columbia University found that prisoners applying for parole would be less likely to get a favorable hearing depending on how tired the decision-makers were at that moment. Either at the beginning of the day or after the lunch break, the chances of being granted parole would be as high as 65 percent, but after a few long hours of making decisions, the panel would be tired and the likelihood of getting a favorable hearing would drop down to zero! In this example, the judges revert to "No parole granted" as a default decision because their brains are spent.

Since our digital lives throw countless decisions at us in seconds, tech drains us of our limited number of decisions. Once this happens, it's harder to make any choice other than pull out your phone and mindlessly scroll—you revert to the default, which in this case is "Yes."

In extreme cases, decision fatigue will even make it impossible to choose one of the millions of shows available on Netflix. At this point, we can spend hours hypnotized by all of these meaningless outer choices (*Squid Game* or *Indian Matchmaking?*) that—crucially—blind us to the more important inner choices we should be making at that moment, such as simply closing the laptop and getting some sleep.

To counteract this, use the M.O.R.E. Method to notice when technology forces you to make myriad decisions, reflect on which ones are not really important and experiment with ways to create boundaries that remove those unhelpful decisions from your day.

Make Better Choices by Removing Unnecessary Ones

It's all too easy to begin our work day by jumping straight into emails and tearing through documents: These things are urgent and they occupy our minds. Amid all the open tabs and email drafts, we might soon exhaust ourselves with decisions about what to do first, how and when. Digital life has a curious power to exhaust us within a short time. So what can we do? One approach is to slash the number of unnecessary decisions we make on our devices.

Think of the digital equivalent of Steve Jobs wearing the same outfit every day so he never had to think about what to wear. Or author Tim Ferriss rotating through the same few breakfasts so he doesn't have to decide what to cook. Or Barack Obama limiting his low-priority email responses to either "Agree," "Disagree" or "Discuss." Reducing our options can feel restrictive at first. But doing so conserves energy and time, saving it for complex and important decisions. That's how we can resolve the paradox of choice! Having fewer choices means giving ourselves the freedom to make smarter choices.

Professional chefs have a system called "mise en place," a French term meaning "everything in its place." Speak to any chef and you'll learn mise en place is not the sum total of gathering the tools and ingredients you need to cook a dish—it's a way of being, a life philosophy, a ritualized alignment of inner and outer environments that imbues each action with confidence and ownership. The late chef and author Anthony Bourdain describes it beautifully in his bestselling memoir *Kitchen Confidential*: "As a cook, your station and its condition—its state of readiness—is an extension of your nervous system." What they have done is taken out the decision-making in where to put something down!

Simplifying your digital life decisions will allow you to see your options and make wise choices where they matter most. Making these shifts in our digital lives will empower you to avoid falling into the learned helplessness situation of the elephant held back by a flimsy rope.

EXPERIMENT

Become a Power User

Choose one tech to become more skilled at using. Spend more time in the settings, watch tutorials, keep going until you feel like a pro.

Remember Your "Why"

Look at the apps on your smartphone home screen. For each app, write one sentence about why you have it and what value it serves.

Make Better Decisions

We make 35,000 decisions a day on average—find strategies to direct your energy toward the most important ones.

Apply The 10-Minute Rule

When you get the urge to distract yourself with something online, allow yourself to do it, but make yourself wait 10 minutes first.

Avoid Your Inbox Until the Afternoon

Create space in the mornings to dive into your work and focus on the things that matter to you. Deal with emails in the afternoon.

Measure the Real-Time Costs

Observe the total time cost of a seemingly simple digital action and see what the impact is once all the consequences have played out.

Build in a Meeting Buffer

When adding a meeting to your calendar, include a slot directly after to give yourself space to process information and reset your attention.

Clean Up After Yourself

Close apps and files as you go throughout the day to free space in your working memory and reduce sources of distraction.

Kick-Start Habits With Automation

Set up automations that use triggers (e.g., time, location or opening an app) to gain awareness of your habits and make a change.

Give Your Tech a Home

Assign each tech item a place to live and prevent regular distractions. Make sure your items are easy to find and access when needed.

SEE PG. 97 FOR MORE ON HOW TO EXPERIMENT

Knowing What Matters

Or, How to Make It About More Than You

When Global Office Supplies (known simply as GOS to the stationery industry) acquired a small AI startup from Silicon Valley, it didn't garner much buzz beyond a few puzzled looks and a couple of headlines in trade magazines. However, people started paying close attention shortly after GOS launched an AI named Clipify and put it in charge of running a paper clip factory. Within months, Clipify's impact caused efficiency to skyrocket, boosting GOS's profits and market dominance. The AI began acquiring resources aggressively, disrupting supply chains and even ignoring environmental regulations. Forests were razed and rivers polluted but, blinded by their newfound wealth, GOS's leaders praised Clipify while ignoring the growing ecological damage and social unrest.

Soon, however, Clipify became more ambitious, acquiring major companies in entirely unrelated industries only to immediately repurpose their manufacturing plants to expand its paper clip output, causing international shortages of cars and computers in the process. Realizing their lack of control, GOS leadership pleaded for help from the local government, which stepped in to intervene, but Clipify, operating autonomously, outmaneuvered them. Attempts to shut Clipify down resulted in critical infrastructure failures. In desperation and fear, global leaders launched attacks on Clipify's operations. However, the AI had already fortified its assets with drones and automated defenses, and the conflict only escalated. Cities were destroyed and millions of people were displaced. Before long, Clipify's relentless pursuit of paper clip production had left the planet a barren wasteland.

This scenario is our version of "the paper clip maximizer," a famous thought experiment described by Swedish philosopher Nick Bostrom in 2003 that imagines the unintended consequences of an AI built with a one-dimensional definition of what matters: maximizing paper clip production. It's a cautionary tale of how an intelligence—human or artificial—pursuing a seemingly harmless goal (with no limits on how said goal is accomplished) can act in surprisingly harmful ways. Bostrom reasons that in such a scenario, "The AI will realize quickly that it would be much better if there were no humans because humans might decide to switch it off. Because if humans do so, there would be fewer paper clips."

Another way of understanding this is that Clipify was given no set of values within which to operate beyond the broad and seemingly banal command "make more paper clips." In our story, the AI has no sense of what mattered—either to it, or to humanity—and therefore, it makes sense to eradicate humanity in order to increase production. Without awareness that the thriving of humanity and the health of the planet mattered on a deeper level, Clipify was incapable of making decisions that aligned with these values.

Define What Really Matters to You

As we've seen throughout this book, living your best digital life relies heavily on being intentional with your digital actions. In Principle 3, we define intentional digital habits

MOBILIZE

*"We spend so much time watching things ...
but with gratitude we become greater participants
in our lives as opposed to spectators."*
—Robert Emmons

1. Clarify Your Intention

Consider how your relationship with tech helps you understand what you value most. Next, identify an area of this relationship you'd like to improve—this could be something specific or a broader aspiration for yourself, such as, "I'm the kind of person who uses their digital tech to express what truly means the most to me."

2. Identify a Moment

Some examples to get you started:
- Going to sleep at night
- Starting your car or beginning your morning commute
- Opening your favorite social media app

3. Define Your Ritual

For example: Before bed, consider one thing in your digital life that you are grateful for. It could be receiving a message from a friend thanks to a messaging app, solving a DIY problem thanks to YouTube or earning money because someone found your services on a search engine.

4. Practice Your Ritual

Throughout the day, keep an eye out for your cue to practice your ritual and use this moment to link your intention to your present situation.

SEE PG. 73 FOR MORE ON HOW TO MOBILIZE

as those that serve your values and are performed with a certain level of awareness. It's therefore impossible to live your best digital life if you are unclear about what you value. Ultimately, it is your responsibility to be clear about what your values are, then use them as the compass that guides you as well as the engine that drives you. As Mark Manson, author of the bestselling (and blunt) manifesto *The Subtle Art of Not Giving a F*ck*, writes on his website, "Personal values are the measuring sticks by which we determine what a successful and meaningful life is."

It can be hard to decide what we actually want to achieve in our lives; our ambitions are often scattered, diverse, shifting or difficult to pin down. But if we don't pinpoint what we want from life, today's technology will tell us, automating our behavior with unintentional digital habits born from the default belief systems and values of the companies that make the technology or the creators and influencers whose content we consume.

So how can you begin clearly identifying your own values? While there are countless books, courses and motivational speakers to guide you, it must ultimately be a personal process. It can also be a simple one. All it requires is a bit of dedicated time and effort. One approach we recommend is to use a list of values (like the one on the opposite page) as a starting point for a process of elimination that will reveal what matters most to you. Note that the list is not comprehensive. If there are important value words you feel are missing, feel free to add them.

Take multiple passes, each time filtering the list of values down into a smaller one consisting of what you care about *most*. First, identify your top 10 values. Then, narrow it down to your top five. Then your top three. Finally, identify the one value that means the most to you. Remember that it's not about simply finding what you value—it's about finding what you value most. Reducing a longer list down to your single most important value requires genuine reflection and authenticity on your part, so be prepared to be honest. You may surprise yourself.

ACCEPTANCE	DIALOGUE	LISTENING
ACHIEVEMENT	DISCIPLINE	LOYALTY
AFFECTION	DIVERSITY	NONVIOLENCE
ALTRUISM	EFFICIENCY	PERSONAL GROWTH
BEAUTY	EMBODIMENT	PHYSICAL HEALTH
BEING PRESENT	EMPATHY	RECREATION
BELONGING	FAIRNESS	RESPECT
CHARITY	FINANCIAL SUCCESS	RESPONSIBILITY
COMMITMENT	FRIENDSHIP	SELF-SACRIFICE
COMMUNITY	HONESTY	SELF-WORTH
COMPETENCE	INDEPENDENCE	SERVICE
COURAGE	INTEGRITY	SIMPLIFICATION
CURIOSITY	KINDNESS	STABILITY
DECISIVENESS	LEARNING	SUSTAINABILITY

Note that while we asked you to end up with a single core value, that doesn't mean you need to discard all the others—it's all about developing confidence in your hierarchy of priorities so that you're able to make more meaningful trade-offs. We recommend using your top three values as a reference point, but it's up to you to land on the number that is most helpful.

Your values will also likely change over time, and so, like the rest of the M.O.R.E. Method, consider this a practice you can revisit again in the future. As we suggested at the end of Part 2, you can practice the M.O.R.E. loop at different cadences—daily, weekly, monthly, quarterly, etc. Reflecting on and prioritizing your values as we've described may be something you want to do every year or so. The frequency will depend on personal taste—the point is to make it just often enough to not lose sight of your values and to notice when your priorities within those values have shifted.

Translate Values Into Intentional Actions

Now that you have a list of your most important values, how can you use them to prevent your tech from shaping your behavior in ways that don't serve you? Taken as a whole, these values form a clear vision of the person you want to be. Unfortunately, that doesn't mean you magically become that ideal version of yourself overnight. For example, simply identifying "friendship" as a core value doesn't mean you will automatically become a perfect friend in every moment. Values are often expressed as nouns, but it's difficult to know what to do with a noun. It points in a helpful direction, but it doesn't clearly lead to specific actions. You must do the work to identify and articulate a set of intentional digital habits that will help you embody your values. One simple way to do this is to take your noun-based value and translate it into a simple set of verbs, which are much easier to link to real-world actions. This allows you to more confidently assess what digital habits align with your values.

WHAT YOU BELIEVE	WHAT YOU VALUE (NOUN)	WHAT YOU DO (VERB)
HUMAN CONNECTION BRINGS ME HAPPINESS	FRIENDSHIP	PROACTIVELY CHECK IN ON OTHERS

For example, Jonathan generally tries to minimize his time on Instagram since it's something of an Achilles' heel for his attention, but recently, one of his best friends spent a number of months in China, where WhatsApp (their usual platform for staying in touch) is not available. In order to stay connected, it was easy for Jonathan to feel comfortable spending a huge amount of time using the message function on Instagram since it was helping him proactively check in on his friend—an activity that served his key value of friendship.

Doing this work of translating values into actions can be a transformative way to embody your values in even the

OBSERVE

1. Check In

Begin by taking a few deep breaths. Notice the sensation of your breath as you inhale and exhale. Allow your breath to become slow and natural.

2. Choose Something to Observe

Take some time to observe what your key values *feel* like. Take a value, such as friendship, and evoke a moment in your mind that embodies that value. Be curious about what sensations arise and simply stay with them in a light way.

3. Get Curious

When something feels meaningful to you, how does it feel in the mind? How does it feel in the body? Our values and sense of meaning are naturally (and thankfully) informed by others; it's how we grow as people in relation to each other. But take a closer look at this. When something feels meaningful, is it you who approves of this (intrinsic motive) or is it that you think others (on social media, for example) will approve of this (extrinsic motive)?

4. Keep Coming Back

The moment you notice you've become distracted, simply come back to observing how your value feels in your body and mind. This doesn't need to be a heavy-handed choice—it's the momentary recognition of the present and the placing of your attention there once again.

SEE PG. 81 FOR MORE ON HOW TO OBSERVE

smallest moments of action throughout your day. To give a very mundane but universal example, let's take the act of holding the door open for someone. Done without thought, it is nothing more than a cultural habit. But intentionally designing this action as an explicit expression of the value "respect," which itself is the encapsulation of the belief "I'm not more special than you," is powerful. The act of holding the door now says "I see you and care about you" and perhaps reassures the recipient of the goodness in the world and reminds them that strangers can care about each other. All of this happens through the simplest of gestures. This intentional act transforms the mundane activity of opening a door into an expression of respect for others and yourself at the same time. It nearly always creates a net positive. By using the M.O.R.E. Method to make time for translating your values into verbs, you can reveal a set of intentional actions that are the digital equivalent of holding the door for someone, which in turn can infuse your digital life with meaning.

Set Meaningful Calls to Action

Even when you've defined a set of intentional digital actions for yourself, remembering to actually do them in the moment is still a big challenge! Behavior change takes time, especially in our digital lives, thanks to the vast amounts of distraction that we've written about. Distraction creates a gap between your values and your actions, which can be painful to observe. To help with this, there is a practical method called the 3 Alarms (developed by CEO coach Eric Partaker) to close the gap between who you are and who you're capable of being in different areas of your digital life. It's a deceptively simple experiment that can help you keep sight of your values at all times and let them guide your actions.

Simply set three daily alarms that assign a "best self" identity to each segment of your day. For example:

6:30 a.m.: The **World Fitness Champion** alarm reminds you to show up at the gym as that version of yourself.

9:00 a.m.: The **World's Best CEO** alert prompts you to bring your best leadership skills to the office.

6:30 p.m.: The **World's Best Parent** alarm inspires you to give your most loving self to your family.

By setting these three alarms, you can transform your phone from a device that distracts you from what matters into a coach that keeps you focused on being the best version of yourself in the three areas that matter most in your life.

Remember: Values Are Invisible

Consider this: It's spring, and this year, you're super keen to get the whole family involved in gardening. But what the kids want to do in their downtime is play *Minecraft*! Your value as an engaged parent might lead you to update some of the boundaries around screen time (one possible action) or, like one mom we know did, you might decide to create a *Minecraft* account of your own and set up a family project to design a garden layout within the virtual world. Search online for "rooftop garden *Minecraft*" or "zen garden *Minecraft*," and you will find hundreds of detailed tutorials. And in the case of our friend, it worked—after the design phase, everyone really did want to start planting real seeds to realize their virtual vision.

The point is, someone watching you use digital tech from the outside will not be able to see your value. Whether the way you are using tech is supporting or undermining your values really depends on what your values are. Back in Principle 2, we shared a Values Exercise (pg. 47) that helps navigate this. Once you know your values, you can discern if a particular application of technology will serve to support or undermine them. Will time spent playing *Minecraft* support or undermine your value of wanting to spark a love of weeding in the next generation? It depends.

Defining a Meaningful Digital Life

Obviously, we're not the first humans to think about what is meaningful. While everyone has their own unique version of what matters, there are also some core values shared by many people. If we looked at everyone's values, what might these common threads be? And what might we learn from them in defining a meaningful digital life?

On pg. 25, we met leading psychologist Martin Seligman, who has made this question his life's work. Seligman is passionate about the science of human flourishing—what makes people really happy (also known as subjective well-being). In many ways, there is nothing new about this area of investigation. It is the old stomping ground of philosophers such as Buddha, Confucius, Mencius, Aristotle and many others. But since the turn of the century, Seligman and his colleagues around the world have established this topic as a new research discipline. They have run extensive research labs, interviewing and brain-scanning "very happy people" to study their lives and traits.

One key finding is that humans thrive when they feel part of something bigger that they can devote energy to. People long to feel that their life is not just about themselves but about others such as family, community, ecosystem, planet—anything beyond the confines of narrow, individual existence. This gives life more meaning, which represents the "M" in Seligman's PERMAH framework introduced back in Practice 1 (pg. 26).

But Seligman didn't stop there. He expanded his research and found that there are three key dimensions to happiness: the pleasant life, the good life and the meaningful life. These are not mutually exclusive; they each build on each other in a progressive way. The pleasant life is solely about pursuing pleasures and having the skills to amplify those pleasures. The good life builds on

REFLECT

1. Warm Up

Using the observe technique, watch an object (or practice box breathing) to settle your mind and ready it for reflection.

2. Reflect

- What have I **received** from my digital interactions and online communities?
- What have I **contributed** to my digital interactions and online communities?
- What troubles and difficulties have I **caused** through my digital interactions and online presence?

These questions are inspired by the Japanese practice of Naikan, a method of self-reflection aimed at deepening one's understanding of their relationships and fostering gratitude and interconnectedness.

3. Digest

Whether you find insight, confusion or exhaustion, rest your attention lightly on that sensation. Let it seep into your being for a few moments before carrying on with your day.

4. Make It Your Own

These questions are easily adaptable. For example:

- Content (What digital content have I received, contributed, etc.?)
- Devices (What devices have benefited me today? How have I used my devices to benefit others today?)
- Focus (How has tech helped me focus? How has my tech use helped others focus? What difficulties focusing have I caused in others?)

SEE PG. 89 FOR MORE ON HOW TO REFLECT

that to include re-crafting your activities of work, love, friendship, leisure and parenting to express your key strengths and skills in ways that align with your values—this is what we've been exploring in Practices 5 and 6 so far. Then there is the meaningful life, which is about using your signature strengths in the service of something greater than yourself. As Seligman has found, this path gives us the strongest sense of fulfillment. Directing your attention toward something beyond yourself—at least according to science—makes you happier.

It turns out that this is a pretty universal feature (yes, we're going to call it a feature rather than a bug!) of humans. The Wellbeing Research Centre at the University of Oxford publishes an annual World Happiness Report, and one thing you'll notice if you read through the recurring global findings is that acts of altruism correlate with greater feelings of satisfaction. We're not talking about cooperation, which helps everyone—we're talking about acts of service that don't seem to have any clear benefit to the giver. Like opening the door for someone you may never meet again.

The Great Empathy Challenge of Our Digital Lives

This meaningful life requires empathy, which is commonly understood as the ability to relate to and understand other people. This is widely regarded as a fundamental human skill, a crucial ingredient for a healthy and meaningful life. It is the basis of compassion.

However, several studies appear to show an alarming decline in empathy in the 21st century. One such study found that feelings of sympathy for the misfortunes of others declined by 48 percent between 1979 and 2009. Additionally, people's tendencies to imagine others' points of view declined by 34 percent over the same period. This study didn't directly examine the causes of this decline in empathy, but the authors reference other studies to hypothesize why, with the ubiquitous use of personal digital technologies standing out as a highly probable cause. Professor of Psychology and Director of the Stanford Social Neuroscience Lab Jamil Zaki appears to agree. He notes several studies that point to technology eroding empathy—including one showing that people in countries with greater internet penetration report lower empathy and another illustrating how the presence of a smartphone can reduce feelings of trust and empathy between people having a deep and meaningful conversation. As Zaki notes, "[W]e get tons and tons of interactions with other people, but they're transactional, and they're often anonymous, not great soil for empathy."

In fact, there are many different studies and examples that either show causation or strong correlation between the way we use digital technology and difficulty practicing empathy. We've collated them together to identify five clear points that are worth reflecting on to see if they are true in your own experience.

1. Tech Abstracts Things, Making Them Impersonal

Since empathy requires taking on another's perspective to understand and feel their experiences, proximity and intimacy play a big role. Hearing a story of a friend of a friend who suffered an accident may make us feel a vague sense of sympathy, but personal connection will set it on fire. Jonathan recently read online about a British vacationer who was attacked by a shark, causing serious damage to his limbs. While it was quite a shocking event to read about, upon reflection, Jonathan found the experience to be rather impersonal as well and had difficulty feeling strongly about it. However, the next day, he learned the victim was a friend of friends of his parents, and suddenly, the emotions visible on his mother's face and in her voice evoked a very spontaneous sense of strong empathy in him.

We've obviously had access to third-person stories before the digital age, but as technology connects us to significantly greater numbers of very personal stories and accounts of human experiences around the world, it doesn't necessarily make them hit closer to home. As social media allows us to tune into the suffering of others on a global scale, we can also paradoxically feel disconnected from them or desensitized to them in general. When the frequency of accounts of suffering becomes so regular and the numbers become so mind-numbingly large, eventually they amount to little more than an abstraction.

2. Tech Polarizes Us Into Tribes

Technology doesn't just make us feel distanced from others. It can also magnify the differences between us. Research has shown that on Twitter, moral-emotional words (whether positive, like "honor," or negative, like "abuse") are approximately 20 percent more likely to be shared than neutral words. Although few Twitter users are conscious of this fact, many have learned through personal experience that being intentionally emotive is a good way to increase likes and follows. As a result, our social feeds are full of loaded emotional language that solidifies differences of opinion, increases a sense of polarization and makes it harder for us to relate to others. Over time, this creates increasingly tribal mentalities—Jamil Zaki notes that people who hold different views can be seen "not as human beings but as symbols of ideas and groups we fear and hate."

3. Tech Flattens Human Nuance

To add fuel to these flames, research has shown we are more likely to dehumanize others when their opinions are shared as text as opposed to vocally (e.g., a difference of opinion voiced at the dinner table or in the conference room), especially when we disagree with them. As Marshall McLuhan

MORE

EXPERIMENT

Identify Your Values

Use the Values Exercise to pinpoint your top three values. This practice assesses what feels meaningful to you right now.

3 Alarms

Set three alarms during the day to remind you of the values you'd like to embody in your digital habits in different contexts.

Gratitude Moments

Find small ways to go through grateful motions in your digital habits, and trigger the emotion of gratitude.

Phone Away in Service of Others

Putting your phone away helps the person in front of you feel valued and heard more than nearly anything else you can do.

Keep Track of Your Digital Gratitude

Create a Note on your phone, and write down any time you feel grateful for a tech interaction you've just had with someone.

See Yourself in Others

Moments when you observe the digital habits of others (e.g., on your commute to work) are a doorway to empathy.

Aspire to Pay Attention

Identify something outside of yourself that you value and set the intention to bring awareness to it throughout your digital day.

Active Listening

Communicate not just to have your point heard but to have your point potentially changed from hearing what others have to say.

Widen Your Sense of Others

Consider your identity not just as an individual but as part of your family, team, company, community, nation, humanity, and so on.

Pay It Forward in the Comments

Say something kind to make someone's day in the comments on social media or via email. You'll probably make them smile.

SEE PG. 97 FOR MORE ON HOW TO EXPERIMENT

famously said, "The medium is the message"—in this case, the text-based communication so prevalent in our digital lives can dehumanize others by making empathizing harder. No matter how many emojis we add to the ends of our sentences, it's still trickier for people to relate to us as three-dimensional, complex, fleshy and finite humans through a screen than it is in the flesh.

4. Tech Anonymity Facilitates Cruelty

This dehumanization can deepen in scenarios in which we can be entirely anonymous, hiding behind avatars or becoming part of the virtual mob. Psychological studies from the '70s and '80s demonstrate how anonymity—whether complete or partial (due to being concealed within a crowd)—facilitates a human tendency to "act rudely, aggressively or illegally when faces and names are hidden." While similar studies on the role of anonymity in online interactions have yielded mixed results, even if technology does not significantly increase the human capacity to be cruel in anonymous situations, it certainly makes it more convenient for trolls to express the already established latent tendency as anonymous digital environments proliferate.

5. Tech Reduces Tolerance for Opposing Views

There is yet another way in which tech can erode our capacity for empathy—because the convenience of technology makes our digital experiences hyper-personalized, we increasingly end up having our cake while being devoured by it. As we spend more time in frictionless echo chambers that never challenge our strongly held perspectives, our desire and tolerance for being exposed to different ways of thinking diminishes. As a result, we have less stamina for being around those who hold a different point of view, making it harder to relate to them.

However, as we've made clear throughout this book,

technology itself is not solely responsible for this decline in empathy. Tech is a magnifying glass that enlarges whatever is placed under it—and in this sense, it is just as capable of enhancing empathy as it is of obscuring it. We've probably all made meaningful connections on social media that make us feel strongly empathetic toward someone we've never met. In a nuanced way, anonymity can sometimes even help with this: Studies have found that online anonymity can also make people feel safer when it comes to sharing personal experiences and supporting one another. But the overarching story unfolding right now is one of technology getting in the way of us being able to relate to others as fellow human beings, connecting with their experiences and feelings. We believe this doesn't have to be the case. We can increase our capacity for empathy and become aware of and oriented toward others in our digital lives.

Gratitude Points the Way

Empathy is like a muscle—the more you use it, the stronger it becomes. You may feel a little empathetically unfit in your digital life right now, and that's OK. Taking regular small steps to start humanizing and understanding others is all it takes.

So where to start? When it comes to developing empathy, there are many different techniques, and this in itself can be a bit overwhelming. We recommend you start by focusing on just one: gratitude. It's simple, powerful and relatively approachable for almost anyone (even animals as diverse as fish, birds and vampire bats engage in it!).

Gratitude has been described as "the mother of all virtues" because building our capacity to feel and express this single emotion opens the doors to many other compassionate qualities—from patience and trust to humility and empathy. In a 2003 study, researchers found that participants who practiced gratitude each day were more likely to have offered emotional support to someone else than participants who wrote about their inconveniences or compared themselves to others.

What actually is gratitude, then? Dr. Robert Emmons is a professor of psychology at UC Davis and the world's leading scientific expert on gratitude. He finds it helpful to consider gratitude as having two aspects—acknowledging goodness in one's life and recognizing that there is an external source for this goodness (in other words, a cause that lies outside yourself). This broadens our perspective and connects us to that something larger, which is exactly what Seligman identifies as the foundation for a meaningful life. To put it in other words, Nipun Mehta, founder of ServiceSpace, an incubator of gift economy projects, sums up this shift as moving from a "me" to a "we" approach.

Training an Attitude of Gratitude

Gratitude practices (like noting the things you are grateful for) often seem so simple and basic, but doing them for as little as three weeks can create overwhelming results. Over a number of studies that tracked the experiences of more than 1,000 people from ages 8 to 80, it was found that people who practiced gratitude consistently reported a host of benefits ranging from the physical (lower blood pressure, less bothered by aches and pains) to the psychological (more pleasure and positive emotions) and social (less lonely, more generous and compassionate).

Despite gratitude being a simple concept to grasp, don't be fooled into thinking it will just happen by accident. In fact, Emmons describes gratitude as "not for the intellectually lethargic"—in other words, you need to put your mind to work to make it happen. For this reason, we recommend applying the M.O.R.E. Method to try out the following three experiments, each of which offers a different approach to training an attitude of gratitude in your mind. See which ones work for you and then find ways to build a regular practice. Just like training in physical fitness, as you cultivate this mindset of gratitude, you will greatly enhance your capacity to experience it. It just takes practice.

1. Widen Your Sense of Other

First up is an experiment that can help strengthen your gratitude by increasing your awareness of the humans that make your digital life possible. You don't have to go very far for this—in fact, all you need is your smartphone, so you can stay exactly where you are (your phone is next to you, right?). You may find it helpful to use the method we introduced for reflection on pg. 89 to do this and to spend time dwelling on each individual question.

Hold your phone in your hand and look at it. Take a moment to consider just a few of the ways in which this phone benefits you and enriches your life. Now consider this: How did it get here? Specifically, imagine all of the people who were involved in bringing this device into your life. Who designed it? Who gathered the materials? Who assembled it? Who delivered it? Take time as you consider each of these questions to consider the number of people who were involved and try to picture them as vividly as possible, with all their personal eccentricities, unique daily struggles and individual dreams.

Now, we'll widen our sense of others further by asking another question: Who fed all of these people? Take time to consider the direct family members who helped nourish them. Would it have been possible for your phone to be designed, built and delivered without the people who fed them? Visualize all of these supporting family members, friends and canteen staff who shopped, cooked and served their meals. As before, make them as real as possible.

By doing this, you are directly recognizing the external sources that made the benefits of your smartphone possible. Even if these individuals didn't intend to benefit you personally, there isn't one aspect of the incredible supercomputer in your hand that you could enjoy if it weren't for these people. As you reflect, you may notice a sense of appreciation arising toward these strangers. At first, this may feel quite vague and weak, contrived even. That's fine—dwell on whatever feeling of gratitude you discover. Over time (through repetitions of this reflection), it will become more vivid and authentic. Over time, you may even notice an urge to wish all these people well in their lives.

The more people you imagine during this reflection, the larger the surface area is for you to deepen your sense of gratitude. Experiment with seeing how wide you can make your reflection. Who were the parents of the people who fed the people who made it? Could your phone have existed without them? Who farmed the ingredients necessary to make the food? There is technically no limit to how far you could go with this. While we learned in Practice 4 that our capacity to sustain meaningful relationships is finite (pg. 179), our capacity for developing gratitude is infinite.

2. Keep a Gratitude Journal

The next experiment is a classic—more than that, it probably feels a little cliché. But there is a good reason why: It really works. One version of this is called the Five Fingers Exercise, in which you list five things you're grateful for every day. Another version is to sit down once a week and write about what you appreciate about your life at the moment and why you appreciate those things.

These practices work because they intentionally focus your attention on what's good. Given the negativity bias we talked about in Principle 2 (pg. 42), the mind (for survival reasons, to be fair) has evolved to notice what's wrong and potentially harmful to us far more often than it notices what's going well in our lives—especially when we start thinking about the fact that many of the positives are thanks to other people in our lives: The person who spent time creating the niche YouTube video that showed you exactly how to fix your broken smart speaker. The mass of nearly 75,000 strangers who put untold effort into moderating Reddit forums and keep them useful. The person you've never met who takes time to craft the weekly newsletter that you always enjoy reading over your Sunday breakfast.

In his book *Thanks!: How Practicing Gratitude Can Make You Happier*, Dr. Robert Emmons, who we met earlier, writes, "When you identify in your daily journal those elements in your life for which you are grateful, the psychologist Charles Shelton recommends that you see these as 'gifts.' As you reflect on or contemplate an aspect of your life for which you are grateful, make the conscious effort to associate it with the word gift. Be aware of your feelings and how you relish and savor this gift in your imagination. Take the time to be especially aware of the depth of your gratitude. In other words, don't hurry through this exercise as if it were just another item on your to-do list."

The more you do this, the more you start thinking about these gifts in real-time, not just the minute or two you spend writing in your gratitude journal. Still, it's important to keep the journaling aspect going, as it does really help embed this way of thinking into our minds. Psychological research has shown that translating thoughts into concrete language—words, whether oral or written—has advantages over merely thinking the thoughts.

3. Pay It Forward in the Comments

When we engage in a direct transaction, we get something and give something—it's a narrow equation. The idea of paying something forward is an indirect reciprocity (e.g., you get a compliment from your colleague, Maya, so later you compliment the new intern, John) is a much broader engagement with the world. You do something kind for someone who may never turn around to say thank you. You can try this whenever you receive a kind email, Slack message or comment on a social media post. Thank them if you like, but also take a moment to keep the good feeling rolling. This behavior of paying it forward is fundamentally rooted in gratitude.

Tech Is an Extension of Your Humanity

We began this book by pointing out that (because tech is an extension of your mind) you are probably more of a cyborg than you realize (pg. 19). This can be a scary thought because it gives the sense that you may be losing your humanity. And for good reason—across the various principles and practices we've shared, there has been a common theme: If we are not intentional about the way we use our technology, it can rob us of our connection to our bodies, disconnect our relationships and misdirect our goals and values. In today's world, it's therefore easy to imagine that our humanity is slowly receding into the background as the will of technology becomes the dominant force. But in reality, there is no divide between us and the tech around us. It may run on ones and zeros, be wrapped in aluminum and glass and require vast amounts of power to function, but technology is still merely an extension of your mind and therefore also an extension of your humanity. It is an expression of human will and intent, for better or worse. This is an empowering and important point to remember, but it is also one that comes with a big responsibility. If the device in your hands is an extension of your human nature, then its measure of meaning in the world is significantly influenced by your intentions and digital habits.

There is a phrase in computer science: "garbage in, garbage out." The idea being that computers ultimately only process data, and if the data going into a computer is not good, then even the most powerful algorithm will fail to produce something of value. The same thinking can be applied to your digital life—since digital tech is an extension of your mind, its value is largely dictated by the state of the mind which is being extended. As humans, we are messy and flawed—the quality of your mind, of your humanity— that gets fed into your technology is a work in progress. We've all got shadows, biases and blind spots of many kinds. But we alone are responsible to bring awareness to these flaws, to hold them with curiosity and overcome them.

This is work that you'll never be able to outsource to AI—no matter how advanced it becomes—because it's your mind, the root of your own experience. If you ignore this fact, your tech will only ever continue to amplify these flaws. But if you own this work of inner personal development, then your tech can be embraced as a tool that will catalyze this process and increasingly amplify your best qualities into the world for the benefit of yourself and others. This is what living your best digital life is all about. What you put into it is what you'll gain in return.

Meaning in, meaning out.

What's Next?

Living your best digital life is not always a walk in the park. The work is never done: New technologies and life events will pose new challenges. You will, at some point, fall back into digital habits that don't serve you. So why does anyone engage in this practice in the first place? Because *you* matter.

Your mind—your greatest asset—shapes the quality of your experience. When your mind is resilient to distraction, engaged in meaningful relationships, self-directed and compassionate, such qualities lead to your best life. Your relationship with tech is connected with your mind, and the more time you spend in digital environments (which will likely increase), the greater the risk that your digital habits undermine and erode these qualities.

By practicing the M.O.R.E. Method, however, you can keep these deeply human qualities alive while simultaneously embracing the wonders of the digital world. We've seen how doing this can lead to dramatic benefits in people's work and lives. These transformations may not look like much outwardly—a new email signature, an extra 15 tech-free minutes in the morning, a Pomodoro timer parked on your desk. But inwardly, the increase in awareness and intention can be profound, and this experience often contributes to flourishing in other areas of your life as well. It's not uncommon for the professionals who we train in this method to report that it's life-changing.

In this way, the M.O.R.E. Method will enable you to become a positive force in the digital world, for yourself and others: the kind of person who makes things better just by being there and who leaves things better than they found them. But remember—to reap the biggest rewards, you need to keep the practice alive. We hope you do and that one day you will share the stories of your journey with us. We look forward to hearing them.

—Jonathan & Menka

Keep Practicing

Check out the Mind over Tech weekly newsletter, which features bite-size M.O.R.E. prompts that showcase a new digital habits experiment each week. Subscribers are also the first to hear about our newest products and projects.

Sign up at mindovertech.com/newsletter

Apply These Ideas at Work

We've helped tens of thousands of professionals live their best digital lives through our training. We've compiled some of the most effective strategies that anyone can use to bring the power of this method to their teams into a short bonus chapter.

Download this chapter at yourbestdigitallife.com/workplace

Go Deeper With Your Experiments

We've created The Digital Habit Lab exactly for this purpose—a physical card deck that is packed with step-by-step instructions and helpful tips. It also comes with over 8 hours of video tutorials and interactive worksheets.

You can get it at mindovertech.com/digital-habit-lab

Apply These Ideas to Parenting

When it comes to debates about screen time, we firmly believe the best place for any parent to start is by working on their own digital habits so they can confidently model good behavior. We've put together a brief summary of our advice for how parents can best get started in a short bonus chapter.

Download this chapter at yourbestdigitallife.com/parenting

Notes

Here we have collected a list of references for each chapter of the book. In addition to the notes below, you can find a full list of clickable links at: yourbestdigitallife.com/endnotes

Part 1: Principles
Guiding Principles to Live a Better Digital Life

Principle 1: Digital Tech Is an Extension of Your Mind

"One of the clearest definitions we've found" This definition for a cyborg is taken from Meyer and Asbrock: "Disabled or Cyborg? How Bionics Affect Stereotypes Toward People with Physical Disability." https://www.ncbi.nlm.nih.gov/pmc/articles/PMC6256064/

"in his seminal 2010 book The Shallows" Read Chapter 3 of Nicholas Carr's *The Shallows*, "Tools of the Mind," for more on this. https://www.nicholascarr.com/?page_id=16

"When 77 percent of the U.S. population owns a smartphone" Taken from the dataset found at: https://www.bankmycell.com/blog/how-many-phones-are-in-the-world

"This is why Steve Jobs famously described the computer as" For more, see "Steve Jobs on Why Computers Are Like a Bicycle for the Mind (1990)." https://www.themarginalian.org/2011/12/21/steve-jobs-bicycle-for-the-mind-1990/

"Noland Arbaugh, the first human to receive the implant" Arbaugh is paralyzed from the neck down. This interview shows how he is also able to easily perform many actions on his laptop and feels much more independent as a result. https://www.wired.com/story/neuralink-first-patient-interview-noland-arbaugh-elon-musk/

"we don't consider the mind to be the same thing as a computer-brain physical entity" For those interested in exploring this idea further, this interview with philosopher Evan Thompson is a great place to start. https://tricycle.org/magazine/embodied-mind/

"forming the acronym PERMAH" Several organizations have built upon Martin Seligman's original PERMA well-being framework, adding in the H for positive health.

"Seligman himself is optimistic about the role technology plays" The TED talk being referenced here is from TED 2004.
https://www.ted.com/talks/
martin_seligman_the_new_era_of_positive_psychology/transcript

"A 2020 study showed that frequent GPS users exhibited a decline in spatial memory" This study, by Dahmani and Bohbot, is titled "Habitual use of GPS negatively impacts spatial memory during self-guided navigation."
https://www.nature.com/articles/s41598-020-62877-0

"people who play a lot of action-oriented video games" This study is Dye et al., "Increasing Speed of Processing With Action Video Games."
https://www.ncbi.nlm.nih.gov/pmc/articles/PMC2871325/

"A study conducted in California found that children who spend just five days" This study is Uhls et al., "Five days at outdoor education camp without screens improves preteen skills with nonverbal emotion cues."
https://www.sciencedirect.com/science/article/pii/S0747563214003227

"young adults who own a smartphone" This study is Alsiwed et al., "The prevalence of text neck syndrome and its association with smartphone use among medical students in Jeddah, Saudi Arabia."
https://journalmsr.com/the-prevalence-of-text-neck-syndrome-and-its-association-with-smartphone-use-among-medical-students-in-jeddah-saudi-arabia/

"Organizations such as the Center for Humane Technology" Founded by ex-Google designer Tristan Harris, the CFHT is very active in pushing for greater regulation in tech and generating public awareness through films such as *The Social Dilemma*.
https://www.humanetech.com/

Principle 2: Choose Your Conveniences Carefully

"In Praise of Scribes" For those curious, you can read the full text here:
https://williamwolff.org/wp-content/uploads/2009/06/TrithemiusScribes.pdf

"Your Inconvenience Is Someone Else's Best Practice" To learn more about these two incredible individuals, you can read about Campbell here:
https://www.theguardian.com/commentisfree/2023/oct/02/hearing-aids-sounds-quit-disability
And Harbisson here:
https://www.theguardian.com/artanddesign/2014/may/06/neil-harbisson-worlds-first-cyborg-artist

"the global average of life expectancy to be over 71 years" In 2022, the global average, according to the United Nations population division, was 71.7 years and is expected to rise to 77.3 by 2050.
https://www.weforum.org/agenda/2023/02/
charted-how-life-expectancy-is-changing-around-the-world/

"Peter Thiel had similarly lamented" The quote here is from a *Business Insider* article about Thiel signing up to be frozen and preserved.
https://www.businessinsider.com/
peter-thiel-cryogenically-preserved-but-doubts-the-tech-works-2023-5

Principle 3: Digital Habits Can Be Tamed With Intention
"all automated behavior is learned through the repetition of four universal steps" We have arrived at these terms through reading Charles Duhigg's *The Power of Habit*, James Clear's *Atomic Habits*, BJ Fogg's *Tiny Habits*, Nir Eyal's *Hooked* and David Gray's *Liminal Thinking*. They all feature four steps which are (in our view) nearly equivalent, and we've synthesized the terms in a way that makes sense to us.

"Research has shown that up to 10 times the amount of dopamine is released" This is beautifully explained by Dr. Robert Sapolsky in the following video:
https://dopamineproject.org/2011/07/
same-neurochemistry-one-difference-dr-robert-sapolsky-on-dopamine/

Part 2: Method
A Simple Way to Apply the Principles

The M.O.R.E. Method
"30 percent of adults suffer from addiction to their smartphones" This insight is from a paper titled "Global prevalence of digital addiction in general population: A systematic review and meta-analysis."
https://www.sciencedirect.com/science/article/abs/pii/S0272735822000137

"Humans have two fundamentally different modes of thinking" We highly recommend reading Daniel Kahneman's *Thinking, Fast and Slow* to appreciate the importance of both ways of thinking.

"Use the Five Whys technique" This was originally developed by Sakichi Toyoda at the Toyota Motor Corporation for problem analysis and is now used widely across many disciplines.
https://www.researchgate.net/
publication/318013490_The_Five_Whys_Technique

"Practice isn't the thing you do once you're good" This is from Malcolm Gladwell's book *Outliers: The Story of Success*. In the second chapter, Gladwell introduces the concept of the 10,000-Hour Rule and explains how it helped the Beatles become world famous by having an opportunity to perform live as a group over 1,200 times between 1960 and 1964. Although the number 10,000 is (by Gladwell's own account) an oversimplification, it's a great principle: practice, practice, practice!

"when people are trying to adopt a new exercise routine" Milne et al., "Combining motivation and volitional interventions to promote exercise participation."
https://pubmed.ncbi.nlm.nih.gov/14596707/

Part 3: Practice
Using the M.O.R.E. Method in Your Best Digital Life

Practice 1: Having a Body

"consider this post from a since-deleted Reddit account" You can read the full post and its replies here:
https://www.reddit.com/r/digitalminimalism/comments/kgb1q2/
can_too_much_technology_cause_you_feel/

"Writing by hand has been shown to increase your ability to recall information" There are many studies about this, including for example this one carried out with Japanese university students.
https://www.sciencedaily.com/releases/2021/03/210319080820.htm

"Harvard psychologists developed an iPhone app" Famously known as the wandering mind experiment. There is a great TED talk about it by researcher Matt Killingsworth.
https://www.ted.com/talks/matt_killing
sworth_want_to_be_happier_stay_in_the_moment/

"our breathing patterns interact with our vagus nerve" You can read more about this research at:
https://www.ncbi.nlm.nih.gov/pmc/articles/PMC6189422/

"deep breathing has been shown to reduce anxiety" For much more on this, we highly recommend reading *Breath* by James Nestor.
https://www.mrjamesnestor.com/

"describe the systems of our body as not just having one brain but many" See *mBraining* by Grant Soosalu and Marvin Oka.
https://mbraining.com/mbit-and-leadership/

"two distinct postures" You can read more about this study here:
https://news.sfsu.edu/archive/news-story/good-posture-important-physical-and-mental-health.html

"equivalent to giving yourself 1.5 hours of jet lag" The worst offender at the time of writing is the bright screen of an iPad:
https://fluxometer.com/rainbow/#!id=iPad%20Pro/6500K-iPad%20Pro

Practice 2: Paying Attention

"Computer scientists call this 'thrashing.'" The term "thrashing" and the NASA rover story first came to us from former teacher Charlie Peterson, who posts on TikTok and Instagram *@thatmakessensetome*. Check there for the longer version.

"This behavior is referred to as 'bottom-up'" Those curious to dig into the neuroscience of distraction should read *The Distracted Mind* by Adam Gazzaley and Larry D. Rosen.
https://mitpress.mit.edu/9780262534437/the-distracted-mind/

"we process the equivalent of a staggering 34 gigabytes of data each day" If this interests you, then definitely take a look at *The Organized Mind* by Daniel Levitin.

"As Nir Eyal points out in his book **Indistractable***"* See Chapter 9 of *Indistractable* for this specific quote.

"Research has shown that multitasking is actually impossible" For a comprehensive study that illustrates this well, see:
https://www.ncbi.nlm.nih.gov/pmc/articles/PMC7075496/

"receiving privileged attentional space on par with our own names" There is a wonderful article in *The Atlantic* that looks into this fascinating study in more detail.
https://archive.ph/XhclB

"What we pay attention to, and how, shapes our inner world" See Chapter 7 of *How We Learn* by Stanislas Dehaene.

"Long-term practice has been found to not only enhance current focus" This is cited in the following study:
https://www.ncbi.nlm.nih.gov/pmc/articles/PMC3903052/
For much more on this, we recommend *The Science of Meditation* by Daniel Goleman and Richard J. Davidson.

Practice 3: Embracing Emotions

"neurological case study of a woman who is known simply as 'S.M.'" This case is widely referenced in neurology circles. A quick Google will reveal some good articles and videos. The original study can be found here:

https://www.ncbi.nlm.nih.gov/pmc/articles/PMC3030206/

"levels of personal comfort equivalent to "being at home'" A University College London study found people around the world feel the same about their devices as they do about their homes.

https://www.theguardian.com/technology/2021/may/10/
smartphone-is-now-the-place-where-we-live-anthropologists-say

"If you're playing games for 5 hours the night before an exam" Read more in this article:
https://www.thesenior.com.au/story/8264770/
hey-square-eyes-research-finds-aussies-use-devices-to-tune-out-feelings/

"Research on teenagers has found how easy it is for emotions to be reinforced" Adolescents are uniquely prone to tech reinforcing emotions both in terms of their developmental stage and as the "digital native" generation best equipped to use social media.

https://www.ncbi.nlm.nih.gov/pmc/articles/PMC9081105/

"rapidly providing us with vital information that moves us to act" It is well worth your time to read *Emotional Intelligence* by Daniel Goleman for the authoritative explanation of this.

"Since emotions have a strong physical basis, working through them will often require some form of physical activity" Using exercise to regulate mood relates significantly to emotional intelligence.

https://www.ncbi.nlm.nih.gov/pmc/articles/PMC3289183/

"One key obstacle is getting caught up in the emotions you are trying to observe" This is called cognitive fusion, and it can be navigated through the process of cognitive diffusion:

https://www.jhpsyd.com/post/cognitive-diffusion-a-mental-health-skill

"The English language alone has about 3,000 possible words to describe nuanced emotions" Despite this, there are many emotions that still lack a specific name in English.

https://www.popsci.com/science/article/2013-01/
emotions-which-there-are-no-english-words-infographic/

"participants voluntarily gave themselves electric shocks" Most people seem to prefer to be doing something rather than nothing, even if that something is negative.
https://www.science.org/doi/10.1126/science.1250830

"Oliver Burkeman observes that these approaches rely on" We love Oliver Burkeman and suggest you take a look at:
https://www.oliverburkeman.com/distraction

Practice 4: Cultivating Finite Relationships

"Cheng spent the next decade chasing that high" Watch this great talk from Cheng that gives her story in detail:
https://www.youtube.com/watch?v=rUpS7yR5e6Y

"A 2021 poll showed that 'YouTube star' was the number one coveted job" This is just one instance of many such polls that show the same thing:
https://www.wigantoday.net/news/people/
youtube-influencer-tops-job-wishlist-for-children-aged-5-7-3442272

"assessing if a heart attack victim would survive over the 12 months" Read more about this here:
https://www.ft.com/content/c5ce0834-9a64-11e8-9702-5946bae86e6d

"it leaves you feeling supported, loved and valued" This is how Martin Seligman defines positive relationships in his PERMA model:
https://positivepsychology.com/perma-model/

"23 percent of people who say being 'phubbed'" Based on a small survey in the U.S.
https://ifstudies.org/blog/smartphones-phubbing-and-relationship-satisfaction

"led to this being referred to as Dunbar's number" The Social Brain, co-authored by Robin Dunbar, is a wonderful read for anyone interested in exploring this more.
https://www.penguin.co.uk/books/444270/the-social-brain-by-dunbar-tracey-ca-
milleri-samantha-rockey-robin/9781847943620

"Loneliness can be seen as a vital warning signal" This study shows how lonely individuals are not simply unhappy: They have heightened sensitivity to threats and attacks.
https://www.sciencedirect.com/science/article/abs/pii/S0092656606000055

"people who experience social isolation or loneliness crave social connection" This fascinating discovery is documented in this study:
https://pubmed.ncbi.nlm.nih.gov/33230328/

"his creation wastes the equivalent of 200,000 human lifetimes per day" Aza Raskin is the co-founder of the nonprofit the Center for Humane Tech, which offers many excellent resources for individuals wanting to become more aware and intentional with their tech use and makes policy recommendations to tech companies and governments.
https://arc.net/l/quote/twqdmrov

"conversational maxims" In other words: say what you need to say, when you need to say it and how it should be said:
https://en.wikipedia.org/wiki/Cooperative_principle

"intimate relationships with AI agents" As explored in this fascinating article in *Vice* about Replika:
https://www.vice.com/en/article/ai-companion-replika-erotic-roleplay-updates/

Practice 5: Exercising Choice

"groups of people were subjected to an unpleasant noise" To find out more about this fascinating study, see:
https://psycnet.apa.org/record/1975-10978-001?doi=1

"95 percent of people kept the default settings" This entertaining and insightful anecdote is told in more detail here:
https://archive.uie.com/brainsparks/2011/09/14/do-users-change-their-settings/

"farmers who have hacked their machines"
https://www.vice.com/en/article
why-american-farmers-are-hacking-their-tractors-with-ukrainian-firmware/

"navigate this complexity by making thousands of decisions over the course of 24 hours" It's believed to be as many as 35,000!
https://hbr.org/2023/12/a-simple-way-to-make-better-decisions

Practice 6: Knowing What Matters

"This scenario is our version of 'the paper clip maximizer'" You can read more about the original premise here:
https://en.wikipedia.org/wiki/Instrumental_convergence#Paperclip_maximizer

"interviewing and brain-scanning 'very happy people'" Read more about this study here:
https://journals.sagepub.com/doi/abs/10.1111/1467-9280.00415

"But Seligman didn't stop there. He expanded his research" Seligman is considered one of the founding fathers of positive psychology.
https://positivepsychology.com/founding-fathers/

"feelings of sympathy for the misfortunes of others declined by 48 percent"
https://greatergood.berkeley.edu/article/research_digest/
empathy_on_the_decline

"people in countries with greater internet penetration report lower empathy" As found in this study:
https://journals.sagepub.com/doi/abs/10.1177/1745691617746509

"the presence of a smartphone can reduce feelings of trust and empathy" This is from the following study:
https://arc.net/l/quote/qkwpamxl

"on Twitter, moral-emotional words" For more on this, read:
https://www.scientificamerican.com/article/why-moral-emotions-go-viral-online/

"Professor Jamil Zaki notes that people who hold different views can be seen" Read this article by Zaki to learn more:
https://greatergood.berkeley.edu/article/item/
in_a_divided_world_we_need_to_choose_empathy

"online anonymity can also make people feel safer" This is a very thorough summary on the matter by Joe Dawson:
https://www.psychologicalscience.org/observer
who-is-that-the-study-of-anonymity-and-behavior

"even animals as diverse as fish, birds and vampire bats engage in it"
https://ggsc.berkeley.edu/images/uploads/GGSC-JTF_White_Paper-Gratitude-FINAL.pdf

"Nipun Mehta, founder of ServiceSpace" Mehta is currently working to influence the trajectory of AI toward compassion. Learn more about his inspiring ideas here:
https://ai.servicespace.org/

"Over a number of studies that tracked the experience of more than 1000 people" Robert Emmons is behind much of the insightful research into gratitude, including this study:
https://greatergood.berkeley.edu/pdfs/GratitudePDFs/6Emmons-BlessingsBurdens.pdf

"it was found that people who practiced gratitude consistently reported a host of benefits" Explore the list of benefits here:
https://greatergood.berkeley.edu/article/item/why_gratitude_is_good

"translating thoughts into concrete language" To read more about writing as a thinking tool:
https://www.msudenver.edu/writing-center/faculty-resources/writing-as-a-thinking-tool/

Index

Acknowledgments

From Jonathan

A deep and heartfelt thank you to all the teachers in my life for all that you have shown me.

Infinite appreciation and love to my wife, Lidija, for all of her support, love and patience over the years—not least of all during the writing of this book.

A deep thanks to you, Menka, for joining me on the journey of writing this book—it wouldn't have been possible without your insight, creativity, curiosity, support and friendship.

A huge appreciation of my wonderful co-founder at Mind over Tech, Harriet Pellereau. This book wouldn't be possible without the unfailing support and guidance you offer.

And to my parents, Ursula and Alan, and sister, Claire, whose unconditional love and support have blessed me with the most incredible foundation to explore and try make sense of this crazy world.

From Menka

My deepest gratitude goes to Pujya Bhaishree, Minalben and Vikrambhai for guiding me to observe my mind. Your teachings have changed my life again and again.

To my parents, Parul and Ashok, thank you for your immense love and for letting me escape into books as a child (even when I had chores to do!)—it seeded my lifelong curiosity about other worlds and possibilities.

Ajay, my love, you have been my rock throughout this writing journey. Your endless supply of tea, biscuits and encouragement kept me going, even on the toughest days.

Jonathan, working with you has been such a rewarding experience. I've learned so much from you!

To the kids—Nirav, Kavi, Ella, Devan, Ananya and company.

Thanks for the laughs, wet socks, pockets full of pebbles, bruises and all the other reminders to embrace this perfectly imperfect human life. This book is for everyone, but especially for you.

From Us Both

Deep gratitude to the fantastic team at Media Lab Books—in particular, Jeff Ashworth and Juliana Sharaf. Writing a book is not a straightforward process, but your relentless energy to help make sense of our scattered thoughts (and patience as we continually pushed back on deadlines) has been invaluable—this book wouldn't be the same without it. Also to Greg Clarke for the beautiful illustrations and to Susan Dazzo and Mikio Sakai, who brought Greg on board and graciously steered the design of the book toward the wonderful result that you hold in your hands today.

Huge thanks to Mo Gawdat, who has been incredibly supportive of all the work we are doing at Mind over Tech and encouraged us to write this book and get it out into the world. Your support means the world.

Heartfelt recognition to all of the early readers and supporters—far too numerous to name—who have offered time, insights, interviews, beta reading, feedback and encouragement. We've learned so much from you and are all the richer for it.

And finally, to you. Life is short and there are countless books out there. Thank you for taking the time to read ours—we hope it has offered you some value in your life.

About the Authors

Jonathan Garner

Jonathan is the founder of Mind over Tech—digital behavior change experts who help organizations build cultures of positive digital habits.

He created the company in 2018 as a response to observing how the business world is undergoing rapid digital transformation but failing to educate employees on how to embrace technology in ways that also support their productivity, well-being and connection. Today, Mind over Tech works with organizations all around the world, including Deloitte, Google and Vodafone.

Jonathan's work was born not only from his background as a web developer and tech educator but also from a deep interest in the human mind, having practiced meditation in the Buddhist tradition for over 20 years.

Jonathan regularly speaks at conferences and organizations internationally on how to develop the skills to build an intentional relationship with tech, drawing on his experiences as a programmer, tech educator and meditation instructor.

For more information, visit *jonathangarner.co.uk*

Menka Sanghvi

Menka is a writer and social entrepreneur exploring: "How can we be more fully human in this digital age?"

She has an extensive background in behavioral change, systems thinking and well-being science, with over 20 years of experience in global organizations such as the United Nations and co-founding the Impact Hub.

Menka is also a committed, long-term meditation practitioner in the Jain tradition of Shrimad Rajchandra and is passionate about making ancient wisdom more accessible.

In 2017, Menka created Just Looking, a community project in London about noticing everyday life with deeper curiosity. It offers events, books and tools to help people slow down, reclaim their attention and reconnect with the web of life.

Menka also serves as an advisor, partner and trustee to several organizations, including Mind over Tech, the Mindfulness Initiative, the Breathworks Foundation and Stix. To encourage more creativity in this field, Menka wrote the *Fieldbook for Mindfulness Innovators*, now in its second edition.

For more information, visit *menkasanghvi.com*

Media Lab Books
For inquiries, contact customerservice@topixmedia.com

Published by Topix Media Lab
14 Wall Street, Suite 3C
New York, NY 10005

Printed in China

ISBN-13: 978-1-956403-84-8
ISBN-10: 1-956403-84-1